Andiamo Le Marche
American Odyssey through Authentic Italy

Andiamo Le Marche
American Odyssey through Authentic Italy

edited by Caitlyn Slivinski

Baltimore, Maryland

Copyright © 2007 by Apprentice House, Loyola College in Maryland

No part of this book may be reproduced, stored in a retrieval system, or transmitted by any means, electronic, mechanical, photocopying, recording, or otherwise, without written permission from the publisher.

Every effort was made to ensure the accuracy of information included in this book.

Cover and book design by Caitlyn Sliviniski
Stories by Berit Baugher, Ann Curran, Chas Davis, George Miller,
    Philly Petronis, Alyssa Porambo and Caitlyn Slivinski

ISBN 978-1-934074-13-8

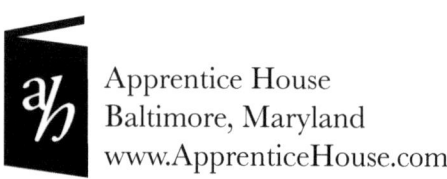

Apprentice House
Baltimore, Maryland
www.ApprenticeHouse.com

c/o Communication Department
Loyola College in Maryland
4501 N. Charles Street
Baltimore, MD 21210

Special Thanks...

This book would not have been possible without the leadership of George Miller under the Institute for Education in International Media. Mark Twain concedes, "I have found out that there ain't no surer way to find out whether you like people or hate them than to travel with them." Hey George -- we like you, thanks for being legit.

Contents

Preface	ix
Introduction	xi
The Events	1
The Landmarks	21
The Lessons	61
The Locals	107

Preface

Welcome to the preface. If you're reading this it can only mean our book sparks your interest, and for good reason. Andiamo: Le Marche is helpful in guiding not only through Le Marche region, but foreign towns in general. A little smile can go a long way and this universal symbol helps navigate our group of four students and a patient professor through several small Italian cities. When a smile doesn't work its magic, funny anecdotes are born which have been compiled into this book.

Le Marche is a true gem. Authentic Italian culture is actively present here because it is virtually untouched by typical floods of tourists. The rustic paradise has an aura rich with tradition. It's this atmosphere plus the balmy climate which initially lures us into Le Marche. Mom-and-Pop shops reign in this region and the aroma of home cooking fills in the air.

Unknowingly, Le Marche provides a therapeutic way of life — it forces you to relax. The shops close in the afternoon to highlight the importance of rest during the day. Have a glass of wine with lunch, walk to work, nap often. These are some of the lessons we learn. Blushing and bellyaching laughs accompany some of the more humbling lessons, of which there are many. The mishaps are raw, sometimes shamelessly awkward, and funny if you like laughing at other people's mistakes. Indulge in this guilty pleasure and take the journey with us. Sweat out the uncomfortable moments and laugh at the confusion as we experience Le Marche and human psyche at its finest.

- Caitlyn Slivinski

Introduction

Take away manmade borders and political conflictions in the world. You're left with a planet – seven continents, one of which is North America. Looking at the United States as just one of seven, why be confined to one country alone? "The World is a book, and those who do not travel read only a page." – St. Augustine

In travel we leave our comfortable homes, our friends, our families and journey out into an unknown world. What makes it worth it? The joy that a destination brings to a person has everything to do with the experience. Learn how people on the other side of the world work and adapt to their environments, the different routes people take. Walk on the same ground historical figures roamed and know you are part of history yourself.

A journey is more than a t-shirt or post-card home, "I was here." Engage in the beautiful affair of travel; see new places and more importantly meet the people that make up our world. Travel creates a hands-on way of obtaining wisdom; immersion provides appreciation for how a society works.

The importance of knowing the world is to see things on a grand scale. It's easy to fall into routine and obsess over work or focus on a small social network. Growing up in the U.S. we learn how to become an adult, to go from point A to point B. There seems only one path to take. In reality we are just a small piece of the puzzle and there are innumerable options in the world. Visiting a destination opens our eyes to the fact that there is more than one way to do things. Life is not a simple math problem. To narrow our options, to think in only American standards, is limiting ourselves. There are endless possibilities of events to fill your life with. Why settle for less than thrilling?

This trip to Italy is an experience that will stay with me always. The people we met and the stories that unfolded are shared here so that others may be inspired to get up and discover their world.

Never set limits. As a child I adored flipping through the pages of National Geographic magazine. I liked seeing pictures of things I'd never get to experience in real life. Or things I thought I'd never experience. I can't remember where or when that idea got planted in my head, but it was wrong. What is keeping anyone from seeing these places, or better yet, being the person taking those pictures? When you read a great American classic, the author was just a person like with a dream.

Designing the Empire State Building, writing lyrics to a national anthem, building a rocket ship, or discovering a new species; who says you can't make the textbooks? The mentality, "History will be good to me for I intend on writing it" (Winston Churchill) is the right attitude.

    Travel leads us to many bumps in the road, but this adds excitement to the adventure. You cannot control everything regardless of how hard you try. Often times these bumps are humbling experiences that help us learn about culture. Enduring the language barrier and unusually hot weather which resulted in constant body odor, we met amazing people that helped us see our old hunk of planet from a shiny new perspective. "People travel to faraway places to watch, in fascination, the kind of people they ignore at home." — Dagobert D. Runes.

    We swim in the Adriatic, sometimes in bathing suits with rented kayaks, sometimes in our dresses after dinner. We ride horses, fearing for our lives as our assigned animal stumbles over roots and down steep hills. We packed into buses filled with people and wonder where these people might be heading -- some to work, home to their families, to the beach, out of town, or foreigners just like us.

    So why do we travel? To reach the top of a mountain and see the view, find a hidden river and let it wash over us, and to connect with people — to understanding someone even though we speak different languages. To dance the night away with perfect strangers that are really not so different from us, that is why we travel.

    Forget thinking outside the box, it's time to live outside the box. Challenging yourself brings forth the best and raises the bar for the next adventure. "The traveler was active; he went strenuously in search of people, of adventure, of experience. The tourist is passive; he expects interesting things to happen to him." — Daniel J. Boorstin.

    - Caitlyn Slivinski

The Events
Activities in Le Marche

- Charming sites at the high point
- Dorks on water patrol
- FORZA ITALIA!
- Get your own bottle!
- How much is that doggie in the window?
- In the end, the right decision
- It all started with the 'fro
- Lost in translation
- Italian boys like American girls
- There's nothing compared to this!
- That horse isn't just standing there
- Too beautiful to take for granted
- Two parties for the price of one
- Would you rather...?

Charming sites at the high point

THERE ARE TWO different parts of Civitanova Marche: the urban, seaport city and the medieval mountaintop village.

The lower portion, the seaport, is an ugly industrial area full of buildings covered in black soot. The city is said to be the place to buy leather goods, especially shoes, but I wouldn't spend much time there. Most of the town was completely destroyed during World War II and the place has been rebuilt for function, not style.

The medieval mountaintop village, a few kilometers inland, retains a certain charm.

You can climb the 14th century walls and look out at the Adriatic Sea from this isolated little hill, the only high ground for several kilometers. The steep streets lead to a central piazza that features a handful of cafes and the stoic-looking San Paolo church.

When we arrived, a few dozen people were anxiously waiting for a wedding to begin. Large, bright yellow sunflowers lined the aisle and the altar of the old church.

Just before 5:00 pm, the guy on the right side of the photo - who has a shaved top of his head but a long mullet and pork chop sideburns - rode into the square on a Harley, screaming that the bride was coming. His gruff voice was barely audible over the roar of the engine.

Then he parked his shiny hog in the walkway in front of the church.

When the bride's limousine finally navigated the narrow, crowded streets and approached the church, the bride - dressed in a modest cream-colored dress - had to walk around the motorcycle.

It was all so romantic.

The crowd lingered outside for a good while after the bride (in the center of the photo) marched down the aisle.

And in classic Italian form, the Harley-riding announcer walked away from the church altogether to have a smoke and talk on his cell phone before the ceremony officially started.

- G. Miller

Dorks on water patrol

OUR STROKES SLOW as we approach the public beach to return our kayaks.

Paddling in our two-seat, bright orange kayak and wearing oversized orange life-jackets, Annie and I become painfully self aware. Our slicked back, ocean-wet hair and grease covered sunglasses only makes things worse.

Out in the choppy waves of the Adriatic the life preservers seemed practical and semi-normal among our fellow boaters. Here in the shallow, waist-deep water near the beach, however, we look like overcautious losers.

As I watch two unsupervised Italian children float by in their inflatable swimmies, I state the obvious, "Annie, I'm so embarrassed."

"I know," she says laughing.

We sit uncomfortably in the boat, trying to muster some sort of dignity before Annie comes to a solution.

"Whatever, just pretend we're important," she says sitting back professionally, scanning the water in mock imitation of a coast guard.

"Over and out bluebird," I say into a fake radio in a low, authoritative state trooper voice. "We got a possible water inhalation at 11 o'clock."

We continue to say nonsense in patrol voices for about 10 minutes before we finally run out of material and decide to paddle in.

It only makes sense that every Italian teenager (and a few Americans) has decided to congregate at the kayak drop off point, to mock the stupid American's floating in.

"You got it from here?" Annie barks deadpan at the Italian man who drags our kayak up to the beach.

Oblivious to our ingenious humor and unable to understand a word of what she's saying he remains silent.

"Just keeping the waters safe," Annie continues as we laugh and trudge through the sand, accepting that it's impossible to be cool tourists.

- Philly Petronis

FORZA ITALIA!

LAST NIGHT THE ITALIAN soccer team defeated Germany to advance to the World Cup championship game. In the picture above, fans celebrated in the seaside resort town of Numana.

- G. Miller

Get your own bottle!

ELLIOTT YANCEY can handle his wine.

He toured the vineyard of Silvano Strologo, tasted a few gentle, dry reds, bought a few bottles and posed for pictures with a really heavy 27 liter monster.

Silvano Strologo - who was nice enough to show us around despite our arriving during pausa - said that he recently sold three of the large bottles to a restaurant in Germany.

Lucky Germans.

The vineyard produces only red wines, mostly varieties of the regional specialty - the Rosso Conero. The grapes are grown across the street from the cantina and you can stroll the grounds at your leisure.

- G. Miller

How much is that doggie?

ON THE DAY WE TRAVEL to Macerata, there is a huge market day going on.

The streets are jam-packed with pushy market-goers and the more laid back strollers who spend hours carefully perusing the stands.

To me, the streets might as well be empty and desolate. I only have eyes for a puppy.

This market looks like the many others I have been to in Italy except larger. Hand-sewn intricate bags hang from hooks next to long, flowing dresses, beside a tent dedicated to belts, jewelry, and hats that range from Viva Italia to the New York Yankees emblem embroidered on the front.

I am bored and long for something new to look at it.

That's when I notice a grungy looking man slumped between two baby carriages. Intrigued, I move closer. Inside each carriage are three delicately small puppies.

Normally more cautious, I barely notice the man who clearly owns the puppies as I dangle my face inside one of the carriages. I ooh and aah over the puppies as they lie sweetly together for warmth and protection. One yawns and stretches his little puppy legs, causing the others to squirm and readjust positions.

"I want one of those puppies," I say quietly to my professor as my eyes remain locked below me.

"Get one," my absent-minded professor says.

He either thinks that I am joking and would never actually buy one or he finds my addiction to the puppies amusing and wonders how far this can possibly go.

"Okay," I call his bluff and run off in search of an ATM.

After withdrawing more euros than I should, I plan on shoving the wad of cash in front of the gypsy man while my professor translates my desire. The puppies' owner explains to us that the puppies were not for sale, and they are actually bait for receiving donations. I figure if I offer more money, then maybe I can slip away with one of these precious looking pups.

Just as my hopes are beginning to soar, the painful reality sinks in: I am returning home to the United States in two days, and I have no idea whether all (if any of my three) flights are willing to accommodate animals...especially animals who have never seen the inside of a veterinarian's office and were purchased from an Italian beggar.

Even if the man lets me buy one of his puppies, I know it wouldn't be the right thing to do, as I probably would have to only say goodbye again.

And so I reluctantly leave the otherwise mundane marketplace with only pictures of the adorable puppies in my memory and on my digital camera.

- Ann Curran

In the end, the right decision

"WAIT," A MAN said in broken English. "Who you pick, France or Italy?"

I am standing in a crowded bar in Cagli surrounded by several crazed soccer fans watching the last minutes of the 2006 World Cup championship game. The game is 1-1 and the overtime periods have not resulted in a wining shot.

The Italians huddle around the TV waiting for the shoot-out to decide the winner. The hunger for victory can be seen in their eyes as they eagerly anticipate winning the World Cup for the first time in 24 years.

You could say I am in a slightly dangerous situation depending upon how I answer the question.

Now, you would think that this was an easy decision. I am in Italy after all, so of course I should want the Italians to win. And I do to some extent.

However, having grown up in a household with a mother who spent her summers in France and a grandmother who was raised there, you could say that I am, in most cases, inclined to chose France when it comes to situations where you are required to pick a country.

And so continues the great debate: who do I want to win the World Cup Finals? France or Italy.

I had visited France several times as a child and have several deeply rooted memories there. But the last three summers I have spent a significant amount of time in Italy, where I also have family, and have grown to love the country and it's people.

"Italy" I answer with a grin and absolute certainty, knowing that I mean it because I truly do want the Italians to win.

I love both countries but the prospect of being in Italy for the celebration afterward is just too tempting.

The crowd roars after the Italy scores the final penalty kick, defeating France, and it brings a tear to my eye.

- Berit Baugher

It all started with the 'fro

LAST NIGHT WAS the grand party to celebrate the completion of the inaugural Camerano Project.

The website is already online and the students are still in Camerano.
Impressive, eh?
Check out the student's work at http://loyolaonline.net/camerano.
For the party at Pininpero, a nightclub on the beach, graduate assistant Chas Davis went all kind of Starsky & Hutch on us.
And that was just the beginning.

Chas broke the ice on the dance floor, shaking and shimmying with student Mark Rowan.

The Travel Girls mingled with the kids from the project.
Jennifer Adams and Averyl Dunn got their groove on.
Then everything went crazy.
Berit tried to drag grad assistant Nikki Luccarelli into the Adriatic Sea.
Even though Berit couldn't get Nikki into the water, everyone else decided to take a swim ...
Including the local Italians, many of whom dipped into the sea in their tighty-whities.
And then they wouldn't put their pants back on (although Allison Fisher, right, didn't seem to mind).
Congratulations to the students of the Camerano Project for surviving and flourishing under extreme conditions.

- G. Miller

Lost in translation

AS WE WAIT FOR literally hours in the Ancona train station for our 13:30 train to Rome, it's inevitable that we become a bit restless.

Our attention is caught when we see a little girl who cannot be more than seven-years old wearing a T-shirt that reads, "Sexy".

We cannot help but laugh.

But then our amusement slowly turns to suspicion and uneasiness.

The dark-haired, olive-skinned girl is traveling with her mother, a younger brother and grandmother and we wonder if her family knows exactly what her shirt means.

The mother seems with it and none of us feels the immediate need to call Division of Youth and Family Services. The T-shirt makes us feel uneasy and concerned for the little girl's living situation.

Is her mother some skeevy slimebag or is the child simply lost in translation?

We hope for the latter and continue on our way.

I guess it isn't much different than seeing a little seven-year old American girl wearing a T-shirt that reads, "Ciao Bella!"

I bought one for my younger sister last year.

- Ann Curran

EDITOR'S NOTE: We recently learned that "Ciao Bella" is the phrase johns use to solicit hookers in Italy. It is also an expression used among close friends.

Italian boys like American girls

Oh, and the photo above is actually from Macerata. We didn't photograph the young girl in the "sexy" shirt
THE WAVES CRASH against the shore while the beat of Shakira's, "Hips Don't Lie," vibrates through the DJ's speakers.

The dance floor is packed with Italians swaying to the beat under the bright Italian moon.
Next to the dance floor stands a bar surrounded by men and women ordering glasses of locally grown wine and shots of Italy's specialty liquor, limoncello.
I make my way toward Philly who is surrounded by admiring men hoping to get a chance to dance with her. We make eye contact and I know that she needs to be rescued.
I grab her hand and we run toward the edge of the dance floor hoping to find our friend Annie.
Philly is glad to escape the persistent Italian men. We spot Annie and the three of us head off in the direction of the parking lot.
Upon locating the two Italian men that brought us, Annie forcefully barks, "Drive us home!"

- Berit Baugher

EDITOR'S NOTE: The exact location of this anecdote is uncertain due to extenuating circumstances. But it was likely near Sirolo or Numana.

There's nothing compared to this!

ITALY PUT THE smack down on France last night to win the World Cup and the city of Cagli erupted.

Sure, it took two overtime periods and penalty kicks but the celebration here in Cagli - as well as across the country - was absolutely insane. Hundreds, maybe thousands of people flooded the piazza. There were dozens of cheering fans in the fountain, flags flying everywhere, a lot of men hugging and kissing each other and a DJ playing the national anthem over and over and over again.

It was the greatest day in the history of Italy since 1982, the last time Italy was the World Cup champion.

Really. Just ask any Italian.

- G. Miller

The Events

Not just standing around

IT'S A GORGEOUS DAY OUT and the sun is beating steadily down on my back, while my jeans are already beginning to stick to my legs.

The scent of hay and manure wafts through the air and in the center of the stables at the Il Corbezzello ranch, the horses mill about, waiting to be assigned a rider.

Immediately upon entering, my friends and I are sized up by the ranch owner Eric and his assistant Donatella. Being only 5'3 and the second shortest of the group, I assume they will fit me with one of the slightly smaller horses. To my surprise - and horror - Eric walks towards the group with the reigns of the largest horse in one hand and his right index finger outstretched in my direction.

"How could they possibly expect me to get on that large creature?" I wonder.

The horse, who's name I was never told, is a black and white spotted pinto. He is fitted with a tan, English saddle and a red saddle blanket underneath. Eric hoists me up and begins to fit my stirrups.

I am overwhelmed with fear. I recall my last encounter on a horse when, at the age of 7, I was nearly bucked off a pony named Ginger. Eric attempts to instruct me on the ways to control the horse. But he doesn't speak English and I don't speak Italian.

I nod my head as he speaks hoping I'll get the hang of it once on the trail.

Early on I am certain that my horse will throw me off. Recalling the stories told on the way to the ranch about people being thrown off of horses, I am overcome with a wave of uneasiness.

As we are leaving the stable, my horse sees another horse and they begin to nuzzle heads. Then they begin making strange grunting noises and all of a sudden everyone is looking at me. Eric is yelling something in Italian.

I am certain this is it.

To my relief, I regain control of the horse and am able to make my way on the trail. We spend the next hour riding through a vineyard and then up the side of the mountain. The dirt paths wind around the various hills and through long stretches of vineyards and thorny brush.

Except for a few false alarms the ride goes smoothly. At some points, the horse seems to be procrastinating. I assume it has a very bad case of ADD but I find out later from my friend Chas - who rides behind me - that my horse is actually stopping every few minutes to go to the bathroom.

- Berit Baugher

The Events

Don't take it for granted

EDITOR'S NOTE: This feature comes from special contributor Chas Davis, a graduate assistant who is currently working in the Camerano Project. He was also a graduate assistant in the Cagli Projects of 2005 and 2006.

WHEN LE MARCHE has been your home for a month and a half, it can be easy to let the extraordinary become mundane.

The quilted, gently undulating landscape seamlessly flowing into the Adriatic below your horse almost seems ordinary. However, the cascading rows of grape vines, the towns perched stoically atop their hills in the distance and the distant chatter from our Italian cowboy guides are reminders that we are no where near the commonplace.

We have traveled halfway across the world to do something many of us could do halfway across our hometowns.

Italy usually brings to mind visions of late-night wine sipping after a day spent touring the marvels of antiquity, not horseback riding. But that's where we are, high on the hills over the Adriatic Sea.

Our horses still respond to the sharp, inexperienced tugs we send down the reigns with head-jerks and indifferent whinnies. The conversations among the Americans still concern trivialities from home.

However, the unfamiliar setting and subtle differences in atmosphere are a constant reminder of how far away from home we really were.

Then, the crises of the moment brings us crashing back to home: I bare the heavy burden of breaking it to my travel companions that Facebook.com is temporarily down.

I hear a cry of shock and disbelief but it's not from our group. It comes from another one of our equestrian voyagers, another young American college student. It was a girl, dressed in jeans and a T-shirt, who could have previously blended in as any other nationality immediately identified herself as one of our countrymen.

"Oh no! Do you have any idea for how long?" she says with a very concerned tone.

I assure her it will probably be short-lived. According to my last visit to our favorite online social network, the system administrators are doing maintenance work while the sun is on our current side of the globe.

We all share in a collective sigh of relief: our link to home won't be permanently severed.

Our thoughts again are focused on riding unfamiliar horses with guides we can't understand, through Italian vineyards, an ocean away from home.

- Chas Davis
chas@creighton.edu

Two parties for the price of one

WE WATCHED THE ITALIANS dance in the street after their team defeated Germany, assuring them a spot in the World Cup championship game.

We laughed and partied and took pictures.
And then it dawned on us: at home, Americans were busy celebrating our nation's 230th birthday.
As historic a moment as it was - the Italians hadn't been to the World Cup since 1994 and hadn't won since '82, we couldn't help but feel a little guilty feeling so connected to a county that wasn't our own.
Especially on the day our patriotism is expected to shine through the most.
It was strange to be out of the county over the Fourth of July but it was an interesting and fun experience to watch another nation's people revel in their own pride for their country.

And even though we were thousands of miles away from home - and craving watermelons, hotdogs and red, white and blue fireworks - seeing how proud the Italians were reminded us that we were also proud of the U.S.A. ... despite our team's performance in the World Cup (America failed to qualify for second round again this year).

- Ann Curran

Would you rather...?

"LET'S PADDLE REALLY HARD so we can get their faster," Berit suggests and we haul-ass to get to the secluded beach, about a half-mile away.

We drag our kayak, which we had rented for 10 Euro per hour from a place called Corallo's, to shore so it doesn't float away. Then, we rip our life vests off and I dive into the water.

"Come on Berit," I yell back to shore but she has collapses into a beach chair under an umbrella instead.

The water is warm with occasional cold spots. I swim to a raft floating a short distance from the shore. Moments later I'm joined by Ann, Philly, and George - my fellow kayakers. Slightly winded from our paddling we catch our breath and sun ourselves on the raft.

"People forget the joy of physical activity like kayaking and bike rides... and eating pistachio nuts", Philly remarks.

We all agree.

Minutes pass and we get into the discussion of, "Would you rather?" This game involves choosing the better of two unpleasant situations.

"Would you rather have a permanent beer belly or only one ear?" Anne asks.

This is not an easy question and the next five minutes are spent weighing out the pros and cons of each affliction. More questions are posed over the next hour or so.

We eventually have to return our plastic, tourist-safe kayaks and we fight the currents back to the main beach.

Back at Corallo's, we decide to treat ourselves to some snacks.

I feel like a kid again when we walk up to the snack bar. I order a caffe del Nonno which I've never tried before but looks good. I've seen it in many shops, its something like a coffee flavored milkshake.

"That's so good!" Berit says, deciding to get one for herself.

It's a small cup but it is thick and has an icy consistency so it lasts. It is very filling.

It's the perfect way to relax after our Adriatic adventure.

- Caitlyn Slivinski

The Landmarks
Must-sees in Le Marche

- Mmmmmm ... truffles
- More than just a transportation hub
- My mouth is on fire!
- The type of town that changes you
- Whoa. That is some pink pasta.
- An uphill climb to see cool caves and more
- Italy in one region
- Accordion-loving Urkel's dream town
- The Jersey Shore of the Le Marche region
- Small but worth a stop
- A thousand years worth of visitors
- In the footsteps of the Roman Army
- A great town when it's open
- Rude girls go hungry
- Four million pilgrims can't be wrong
- A secluded beach that's worth the hike
- Mountains of possibilities
- Sky high and loving it
- Everything from necklaces to Nutella
- Princess for a day?
- Landmark tower leads to nude beach!
- Home of the poet Leopardi
- Land of velvet beaches
- Sparky watches the world
- Jewel of the Conero Riviera
- In the heart of white wine country

Mmmmmm ... truffles

BELIEVE IT OR NOT, Acqualagna is a rather famous place.

Set in the rolling foothills of the Appenine Mountains, the city is the world's Mecca for truffles.
Founded in 1292, the small city of 4,000 people plays host to multiple truffle festivals annually in February, August and November.
Farms abound in the region, instilling the feeling of old world Italy there.

- G. Miller

My mouth is on fire!

YES, THERE IS A FLAME in Kaitlyn Massimino's drink.

The drink is one of the house specialities at Caffe del Corso, the happening spot in the center of Old Cagli. On an average weekend night, the bar/ restaurant is jammed with revelers drinking and dancing to the latest sounds.

And the man behind the bar is the reason for alll the good times.

His name is Luca but they call him Seven, a reference to an old family nickname. He is huge, happy and full of tattoos.

Ask for a shot and he's likely to do one with you. His brother, Eddie (another nickname), is likely to grab your girl and spin her on the dance floor.

After one night in the bar, you are like family.

- G. Miller

(the photo of Seven comes courtesy of 2006 Cagli Project member Lizz Samolis)

Transportation hub and more

IF YOU'VE TRAVELED THROUGH Italy, you most likely associate the city of Ancona with transportation.

As travelers, me and my friends have probably spent the most amount of time in Ancona anxiously waiting to leave: our four hour train to Rome, our overnight ferry to Croatia and our multiple bus trips home to our apartment in Camerano.

However, it isn't until a day trip devoted to the city itself, that we realize the historic sites, architecture, views, cafes and shops are worth at least a day of exploring.

Driving into the city, we are naturally drawn to a large dome at the top of a hill overlooking the Adriatic Sea. Following sporadically placed arrows, we wander up the Colle Guasco hill, tripping over random cobblestone streets, lingering under stone bridges and climbing steep steps to reach the peak.

At the top, I can see that the 300-foot dome is part of the Cathedral of San Ciriaco. Drenched with sweat and panting, we walk past two stone lions through the Cathedral's Gothic style door, only to be kicked out by an old Italian man who scoldingly points to our tank tops. If we had been covered, we could have seen the crypts inside that contain the remains of a temple from the third century B.C.

Dehydrated from our hike up, we walk down the street a little ways to a small café appropriately named Bar Duomo. Terrace seating with a nice breeze and beautiful views of the Adriatic Sea makes it an ideal spot to rejuvenate with a gelato or cold drink.

"What should we see in Ancona?" I ask our waiter.

He leads me to the café's side balcony and points to Ancona's main landmarks in broken English. Looking out at the city, I can't distinguish any lasting destruction from WWII bombings or damage from a large earthquake in 1972.

From my many bus trips I recognize the Arch of Trajan, a 61-foot high marble arch bordering the Adriatic. Further from the sea, at the base of the Colle Guasco hill the waiter points to an amphitheater and a lighthouse on an adjacent hill in the

Parco del Cardeto.

Both sound interesting and look within reasonable walking distance. After a drink, we decide to descend Colle Guasco to get a better look at the amphitheater.

The "amphitheater" is a disappointment. Surrounded by a metal fence and overgrown with weeds, the crumbling form of what was once an impressive public venue in the first century AD, now looks more like a zoo exhibition.

Ready to redeem ourselves, we head towards the lighthouse at the top of another hill. At street level it is difficult to get our bearing so we ask a couple of Italians in the street where to go. Doubting our vague directions, we walk past residential house's driveways to a dirt path. Despite some intimidating signs signaling that we are on Military Property, we continue to a modern lighthouse, built in 1970. Beyond the modern lighthouse is an original 1860 lighthouse donated to the people of Ancona by Pope Pius IX.

It is somewhat disappointing to discover that the lighthouse is not open to the public but the peaceful scenery is worth the trip alone. Free from the crowded streets and noises of buses, trains and ferry whistles, a solitary wooden chair that overlooks the Adriatic Sea provides the perfect seat to detach from city life. A poster on a closed snack shop front informs visitors of summer night concert dates performed on a small stage adjacent to the lighthouse.

Besides the historic sites, Ancona also has some worthwhile modern attractions. There are a couple shops like Zara, United Colors of Benetton and Max & Co that have reasonable prices and a wider selection of cute clothing compared to their American branches.

On Tuesdays and Fridays, Piazza d'Armi has an open market from 8 to 12 and Corso Mazzini has one everyday except Sunday where you can pick up inexpensive clothes, knick-knacks, and souvenirs. After shopping, various piazzas' around the city, sit at a café and people watch amidst 16th century architecture and statues.

Rather than a destination, people usually think of Ancona as merely a stop off point, the beginning or end of various bus, train, ferry or plane trips.

Instead of sitting in a station you should take a look around.

- Philly Petronis

A town that changes you

EDITOR'S NOTE: Today's essay comes to Andiamo courtesy of Kevin Zazzali, a member of the 2006 Cagli Project.

WHEN AMERICANS TRAVEL TO ITALY, they usually head for Bologna, Florence, Naples, Rome and Venice.

So when I arrived in Cagli, a small town in Italy's Le Marche region, I dropped my bags in my apartment, stepped outside and scratched my head trying to answer the question, "What the hell am I doing in Cagli?"

I was there for an extremely compressed study abroad program but ultimately concluded that Cagli should be added as a contender for one of the best destinations in Italy.

Even though it is small, (only about 10,000 Cagliesi populate the town) Cagli has a long history. The huge stone Torrione was built by Giorgio Martin in 1480 A.D. Cagli has nine churches, a palace and four different gates, or entryways, to the city: Porta Flaminia, Porta Lombarda, Porta Massara and Porta Vittoria.

Any traveler eager to experience a dose of old-school Italian living should book a weekend at Casale Torre Del Sasso (which loosely translates to, "village tower of the stone"), one of the many agriturismi springing up in Italy. I spent two nights there with my family. Casale Torre Del Sasso is reminiscent of a small castle-like embattlement situated at the top of a steep hill. Mario Carnaci runs the agriturismo.

The exterior is deceiving. The first floor is full of antique furniture generations old that makes a person feel warm and at home. There are windows everywhere, a fireplace, a sofa and plenty of room to stroll around and examine the antiques. Two queen-sized bedrooms contain all the accoutrements any American tourist would need, such as a huge sink, mirror and bathtub.

After settling in, take my advice and ditch your car or van and lace up your sneakers. Take a left leaving Mario's Torre Del Sasso and start experiencing Cagli! A steep hill will take you to your first adventure: a tiny path leads to a bridge that resembles the one from "Indiana Jones and the Temple of Doom." The steps are made of wood and, although metal cables suspend the bridge, some steps are missing. The view is mesmerizing during the day, but be careful walking at night.

Definitely book a dinner at the classy La Gioconda on Via Brancuti, (a side street directly off of Via Leopardi). With reservations, you will be seated immediately. Try the pasatella in crema di formaggio e tartufo nero as an appetizer. It is pasta served in a light cream sauce, topped with black truffles. It is filling, although with a strong aftertaste. For a second course, stick with your American instinct and select the salsiccia e cipolla grigliata. This dish contains perfectly grilled sausages and onions that are served in a delicious olive oil.

Get a good night's sleep and start the next day right with a coffee at the Caffe del Commercio, in the Piazza Matteotti. The piazza is the best place to get to know and observe the Cagliesi. Whip out your dictionary and say hi to Mimi, who owns the caffé, or any of the other kind employees, such as Dodo and Marina. They love speaking to Americans and will remember your name. I mentioned the name of a friend who had traveled to Cagli three years ago on my first day in town, and they immediately warmed up to me.

Then walk off the croissants you ate and visit the waterfalls of Cagli. From the piazza, take Via Leopardi and make a right on Via A. Celli, which will take you close enough in the direction of the waterfall. After a 15-minute walk, the rushing sound of the light blue water will greet your ears before you see the falls. Walk slowly and safely, because a hidden path takes you to a steep descent. The effort is worth it, because the falls are secluded, clean and can act as your private swimming pool under looming Monte Petrano. Bring a towel and sunscreen if planning on staying more than an hour.

Spend the rest of your second day visiting the shops of Cagli. Buy a "Shark Kong" T-shirt next to the gold jeweler's shop on Porta Vittoria and have fun explaining why Italy combined King Kong with a shark. I still have not figured it out. Then grab a panino at Caffé d'Italia. Ask to see the opera schedule in case an opera is being performed at the Accademia Del Teattro

Instead of a night at the opera, you might want to barhop a little. First, head outside the piazza and order the McCain Pizza, which is a plain pizza topped with fries (yes, French fries!) and a few drinks at Squa Qua, on Via Leopardi to get warmed up. Wander across the street to the local wine bar, Caffe' del Corso, which is owned by a big, burly, friendly guy named "Seven."

While there, treat yourself to a Devil's Kiss beer. This is a German beer boasting 8 percent alcohol that will surely please any college student. Then stand on the street with the Cagliesi. One will surely approach you asking, "Americano?" If you're not tired, start talking and see what else you can find out about Cagli. Once you return to your temporary home at Casale Torre Del Sasso, you can relax in the mini courtyard or by the pool if the weather is warm.

Although 20-plus journalism students descend yearly upon Cagli, the town is a find for any traveler looking to get away from the bustling markets of Florence (and via two trains, it only takes about three hours with one connection).

Cagli is the type of town that changes you.

For a rookie journalist who hated traveling until about three weeks ago, I am already figuring out how to extend my stay in Italy. Rome did not do that to me. Venice did not do that to me. The beauty, sounds and overall peace of Cagli, however, did. If you take a risk and book a weekend at Casale Torre Del Sasso, and greet Cagli with an open mind, you will be rewarded with the type of experience you would never get in a big city.

Come to Cagli and you will understand why I stopped scratching my head the first day of my four-week stint here.

If You Go, Don't Miss:
- Accademia Del Teatro
    - Tel. 0721-787644 (9:30 a.m. – 12 p.m.) and 0721-781341 (5 p.m. – 7 p.m.); www.accademiadelteatro.org; accademiateatro@libero.it
- Caffe d'Italia
    - Piazza Matteotti, 3. Open 9 a.m. to 1 p.m. and 4:30 p.m. to 1:00 a.m. Seven days a week.
- Caffe del Commercio
    - Piazza Matteotti, 18. Open 11 a.m. to 1 p.m. and 4 p.m. to 2 a.m. Tuesday through Sunday. Closed Monday. Tel. 0721-787220.
- Caffe' del Corso
    - C. XX Settembre, 5-7. Open 12 p.m. to 4 p.m. and 7 p.m. to 3 a.m. Tuesday through Sunday. Closed Monday.
- La Gioconda
    - Via Brancuti. Open 12 p.m. to 5 p.m. and 7 p.m. to 11 p.m. Tuesday through Sunday. Closed Monday. Tel. 0721-781549, www.ristorantelagioconda.it
- Squa Qua
    - Via G. Celi. Open 11 a.m. to 1 p.m. and 4:30 p.m. to 1 a.m. Seven days a week. Tel. 0721-790418, www.squaqua.it or info@squaqua.it
- Torre Del Sasso www.ware.it/Agritour/Marche/Pesaro/TorredelSasso/eindex.htm
- The Waterfalls!

Internet Spots:
- B.T. Point
    - Via Mameli, 7. Open 9 a.m. to 12:45 p.m. Tuesday through Sunday. Closed Mondays.
- Squa Qua

- Kevin Zazzali

Whoa. That is some pink pasta.

IL CORBEZZOLO SMELLS like Le Marche.

The agriturismo - a bed and breakfast type establishment with a restaurant featuring traditional, regional dishes - has a horse farm and is surrounded by vineyards and farm land.

The scent of hay and horses wafts through the air. If you study the local wine - the Rosso Conero - you can almost distinguish the same smell in your glass as you can at the agriturismo.

That is not a bad thing.

But the little establishment takes the specialty wine one step further. They have used that Rosso Conero to add color, literally, to their pasta dishes.

It can be a little shocking.

Photography instructor David Maialetti received his plate of pink raviolis with a look of awe.

But he ate them. And they were good. And filling.

- G. Miller

An uphill climb to cool caves

ARRIVING IN CAMERANO, riding in a large turquoise van, one of the first things that is pointed out is the playground bar.

At first I think I've misunderstood.

We pass by and I see a children's playground and something that looks like a snack bar in the corner of the park.

"Playground bar?" I say in confusion to Philly, my colleague on this program. She nods back and I start to wonder what kind of town is this that I will be living in the next four weeks.

My next observation is the hills. If your parents are like mine they love to remind you that when they were you age they had to "walk to school uphill, both ways."

I used to laugh at such a thing, but now I feel like I am experiencing just that. It seems everywhere we go is uphill. It's no wonder that of the 4000 people living in Camerano most of them are physically fit, despite the overly available gelato.

We finally arrive at a row of apartments that will be my new home. Our driver Marco Bravi squeezes our Scooby Doo mystery machine look-a-like car into a parking spot between the smallest car I've ever seen and a Vespa. These two vehicles would be a common sight from now on. Walking up three flights of stairs I hear the lock click and the door swings open to our apartment.

Our purple apartment.

There is a poster of Vespa's on the bathroom door. The Kitchen is orange. These bright colors are typical decorating for Italians. There is no dishwasher, we wash dishes by hand. We have a washing machine but it's broken and so we do that by hand too and hang it on the clothesline to dry. I feel like I've gone back in time instead of to a different country.

But it is just a different country and these surprises in my apartment wouldn't be the only ones in Camerano. Many other hidden secrets lay throughout this town and the only way you could ever find them is to talk to the locals... or read this.

The most wondrous of Camerano's unknowns is the network of caves that is carved beneath the entire town. Walking into a store in the middle of town you would never guess that it contains a secret door that is an entrance to caves hundreds of years old.

The caves are a chilly 55 degrees, give or take a few degrees. This is due to the depth which can be up to 60 meters deep. A sweater is definitely advised. The tunnels range from very narrow with low ceilings where you have to duck your head if you over five feet tall to large rooms that could hold a hundred people. There is evidence that some rooms held mass when religious freedom was restricted by the town's occupiers.

Camerano was founded by the Piceni tribe in about 600 BC and since then there have been many turnovers in rulers.

During WWII the Germans occupied Camerano and the citizens used the caves as a safe-haven from Allied bombing. The elder Cameranesi tell their grandchildren stories of living in these caves. At one point the citizens of Camerano were forced to retreat to the safety of the caves for eighteen days straight. Looking around the caves, with rough jagged rock in some areas and no privacy not to mention the areas that drip water, it is almost unimaginable to think about having to live there for almost three weeks.

There are large decorative arches carved into in the room walls and smaller arches which held lanterns to illuminate the temporary abode. One room is intricately carved in a fashion so that when one stands in the exact center and speaks it sounds as though you are hearing your voice in headphones.

The caves, since originally dug, have been repaired for the safety of visitors. Brick walls have been raised to make sure the ceilings don't falter and arches have been given extra support with brick as well. Although these addendums are rather unsightly it's worth it so the history of these remarkable caves is not lost.

Other stones have also been brought into the caves, but not for support. The original caves were connected through many tunnels which lead up to the basements of several homes in the center of town. Since then the Camerano citizens have built stone walls to close off the tunnels to use the portion of the caves that lay under their homes as personal storage space such as wine storage.

Emerging from these caves you are faced with a beautiful view of the Adriatic Sea. Camerano sits in close proximity to the Conero Peninsula which is a coastal terrain with added culture because of the roman ruins and history that lay within. A twenty-minute bus ride can deliver you right to the shores of Numana, one of the nearby beaches. The last bus brings you back to Camerano at 8pm, which means if you don't have a rental car you'll be spending your evenings in Camerano.

There is a piazza in town, although it is rather small and lacks typical nighttime activities. The senior locals tend to gather here, men on benches and the women linked arms and doing laps around the perimeter of the piazza. This can be seen any day of the week but if you want to hit Camerano's nightlife you need only walk down the street where you'll find an outdoor corner bar with view of the sea, a pizza restaurant/ bar and a club.

After that there doesn't seem to be much going on in Camerano, but with the right people, these few watering holes are enough. The pizza place doubles as a gelato hotspot and only €1.30 can buy a small scoop of heaven. During the day you can get pizza, salad and cold drinks there and it is one of the few places that stays open during pausa.

As far as sight seeing goes in Camerano you won't want to miss the San Francesco church with famous painting of Loreto. It has a crypt that's closed up and doesn't have much appeal from the outside is a gem inside. For those sports fans there is a stadium located in the southeast corner of town. Supermarkets are all around but never open, or so it seems (they all shut down for pausa from 12:30 until about 5). The G&S has the most selection, but it is quite a hike from the center of town and on the hot July days in Camerano, trekking uphill with a full load of groceries can be a task and a half.

Trattoria Strologo, Osteria Kren, Hotel 3 Querce and Piccolo Mondo are restaurants we visit when we're too lazy to make the trip to the market.

To get your political fill, tours are available in the City Hall and if you're lucky you can meet with the mayor and ask question such as the effect the new Ikea will have on the traffic around the Camerano area.

- Caitlyn Slivinski

Italy in one region

WE DROVE TO THE far western reaches of the Le Marche region to find a restaurant.

It took forever to get there but it was worth it.
They say that Le Marche is Italy in one region and there appears to be some truth to that.
We began our day in Camerano, near the beaches of the Conero Riviera, and wound up in the glorious mountains of Central Italy. In between, we passed vineyards, ancient villages, farms of all sorts and modern, industrial centers.
When we finally arrived in Castel Sant Angelo, the sun was setting over the region, casting an orange glow over the world. It was beautiful.
This image was taken in front of Il Giardino degli Ulivi, the restaurant we drove hours to find.
The eatery was a real treat and it deserves its own entry. So keep your eyes open ... it will come in a few days.

- G. Miller

Urkel's dream town

IT'S ONLY TWO EUROS.

Am I really willing to take the time and waste the cost of two glasses of wine to tour a museum devoted to accordions? When or where else will I ever have the opportunity to go to an accordion museum, let alone think about such an instrument for longer than 5 seconds? My internal debate comes to a breaking point as the man at the front desk stares at me expectantly.

I splurge.

My skills communicating with Italians are reliant on hand gestures and English heavily laced with Italian accents I've picked up from Olive Garden commercials and spaghetti eating cartoon characters. My request for an entry ticket is answered with an equally difficult to decipher response from the man at the front desk. He guides me to a flat screen TV and assures me that a film will begin with English subtitles.

It is a short film with enough retainable facts that could start a couple of interesting conversations or at least impress some lonely Berkeley college musician cornered at a bar, such as fact that it takes over three months to create an accordion with over 15,000 pieces. As I watch the delicate, time consuming tuning process done by filing fractions of a millimeter off each individual reed, I can understand how the accordion came close to extinction due to the electronic music boom of the 20th century.

Once the film ends after about a half hour I walk around to look at the glass cases displaying various models of accordions dating from present day back to the late 1800's. It is said that the first accordion created in Italy was in the town of Castelfidardo in 1863. A separate room is entirely devoted to paintings of accordions and accordion knick-knacks from glass figurines to a random bag of accordion shaped pasta.

Just as I am feeling sorry for the compiler of such obscure objects the sound of a live accordion fills the museum. I walk into the back room and see the man who gave me my ticket smiling and swaying as he plays a piece that reminds me of Lady and the Tramp.

An Italian family with three kids surrounds him taking pictures and clapping along. When he finishes, we all shout, "Bravo." At two euro, the live performance was a good deal.

- Philly Petronis

The Jersey Shore -- Italian style

SCREAMING KIDS, NAGGING PEDDLERS, wafts of fried food and the obnoxious horn and calls advertising fresh cut coconut are all part of the experience at the Fano beach.

The shallow water that remains at knee level for about a quarter of a mile makes it an ideal beach for kids and people who fear the depths of unknown seawater.

For only 6 euros anyone can rent a lounge chair at one of the various beach sections. The adjustable sun shield on top of the chairs makes the fee seem worthwhile in the long run compared to the price of wrinkle reducing Botox.

To stock up on beach gear there are shops along the beach nestled among endless restaurants and gelaterias. Homesick American's can find refuge at the Beach Burger, a fast food hamburger joint with a fluorescent and turquoise based décor reminiscent of The Max restaurant from Saved by the Bell.

You expect to see Zack, Slater, Kelly, Jessie, Lisa and Screech sitting at the next table.

A little farther off the main sidewalk is an excellent Spanish restaurant, Buena Siesta. They serve various salads and piadine – flat bread – sandwiches. A basket of chewy hot piadine is served with every salad and is tasty enough (to us at least) to motivate a return trip from the previous year.

If for no other reason, a visit to Fano is worthwhile for the people watching alone. We noted that Fano's boardwalk was unlike the popular beach towns in Le Marche in that it's as busy during the prime beach hours as it is at night.

Sitting at a café along the boardwalk is like watching a runway show. As the sun sets, men's gold chains and Speedos are exchanged for wife beaters and skintight jeans. Scandalous bikinis are replaced with skanky mini skirts and midriff revealing tops.

I was only slightly skeeved out by the man who was hanging out his hotel window, paparazzi zoom lens camera in hand snapping away at the passing nightlife below.

Who could blame him?

Some of the outfits that we saw preteens wearing as they walked along the boardwalk would put Tara Reid to shame. The outrageous clothes, excessive makeup, gold jewelry made us all agree that Fano is essentially the "Jersey Shore" of Le Marche.

If you want to get away from the younger crowds, loud music and bars, follow the signs to "Centro." This offers a more relaxing setting for a night with low-key bars and excellent restaurants with outdoor seating. During the day and early evening, there are a wide variety of clothing shops and cafes.

- Philly Petronis

Small but worth a stop

THE AREA AROUND FERMINGANO is industrial, with large factories scattered along the road leading into the city.

And the town itself is tiny, with a small piazza and a handful of streets full of ancient homes.

But the tower and bridge that runs across the Metauro River is a sight to see.

From the city, you can walk across the bridge to, well, nowhere. It merely takes you towards a parking lot and a main road. But while you are on the bridge, the water flows beneath your feet and down a small set of waterfalls. From the main road, it is beautiful to see.

Abandoned factories line the river in the city, offering signs of why this place came to be: its great location.

It is also on the road to Urbino, the provincial capital. So if you are on your way to Urbino, stop off and see the wonderful town of Fermingano.

It won't take long.

- G. Miller

Visitors for a thousand years

BURROWED IN THE MOUNTAINS near the massive Monte Catria, the monastery of Fonte Avellana (the hazelnut fountain) has been a magnet of Catholic studies for over a thousand years.

Founded in the 900's AD, the hermitage quickly became a model of monastic life. It is mentioned in Dante's Divine Comedy, it was sacked by numerous invaders over the years and it was suppressed by the newly formed Italian state in the 1860's.

Pope John Paul II visited Fonte Avellana in 1982 and elevated the church there to the status of Minor Basilica.

The facility survives today and is open to visitors. It is difficult to find, far removed from other tourist attractions and not really near any large cities. It is relatively close to the impressive hilltop town of Frontone but even that is several kilometers away on a long, winding road.

The grounds at Fonte Avellana are beautiful and there is a lot to see in the actual structure, from the large library - dedicated to Dante - to the crypts and the 12th century church of Santa Croce and Sant' Andrea.

There is also a restaurant and a gift shop on the property and an agriturismo just up the hill.

- G. Miller

Roman Army footsteps

THERE WERE ONCE four main roads leading to and from Rome.

They were routes used by the Roman Army in ancient times to get from Rome to other sections of the empire.
The Via Flaminia was the Roman road to the Adriatic Sea with the road finally ending at the seaport of Fano.
To get to Fano, however, the Roman Army had to trek through the steep and treacherous mountains, following the Burano River for much of the journey.
The easiest path led the Romans through the Gola Del Furlo, the throat of Furlo. But even that was not an easy path. The Romans had to dig a deep, 30 foot long tunnel through limestone hills.
Today, drivers still use that tunnel when driving through the scenic range that is remniscent of the Grand Canyon.

- G. Miller

A great town... when it's open

THE NINE BENCHES IN the main Jesi Piazza remain empty.

Their dark brown wood has absorbed the midday sun, making them too hot to lounge on comfortably. Anyone still out remains under cover in alcoves or in the shade of shop awnings.

White "saldi" signs tempt lingering shoppers to search through the glass windows for mid-summer deals. The sound of jangling keys and the clanking of rolling metal blinds covering closed shop fronts is replaced by clattering plates in nearby cafes.

Families of tourists clad in comfortable shoes and casual clothes, swing shopping bags, as they wander around trying to find a place to eat.

One by one shopkeepers walk slowly to a rusty bike rack to unchain their transportation and pedal home for lunch and rest.

Large clock hands on the top of the Teatro Pergolesi remind Jesi that it is one o'clock, the start of pausa.

- Philly Petronis

Rude girls go hungry

IT'S SATURDAY, THE FIRST day of July, and the first thing on our mind after arriving in Camerano is getting some food.

Quickly we find a pizza place called L'Altro Mondo and Philly and I order a tomato and mozzarella panino (sometimes called panini's back home) to share. It's our first dinner in Italy and wouldn't you know it, our much anticipated panino arrives and it's not, well, "panini-ed".

This doesn't stop us from eating it, but it's easy to understand our disappointment when we were expecting a flattened grilled sandwich with steaming slices of tomato and melted cheese and instead receive slightly toasted bread with lukewarm mozzarella and cold cherry tomatoes.

We might have given up on the restaurant right then and there had it not been for our American peers. They are sitting at our table and are wise enough to splurge for a pizza pie. It looks tasty. Jealously, we watch each slice disappear. We sit for some time scrutinizing the girls' facial expressions in an attempt to decipher just how good the pizza tastes.

Deciding the pizza is palatable we take a break from staring at our fellow diners and spend the next moments casually insulting each other.

"I'm hot."

"Shut up Berit, you're such a whiner."

"I know, I'm the whiner," Berit answers. "Caitlyn's the communicator, Philly's the smart one, and Ann is the bitch".

"Hey, I'm not the ..." Ann says but stops herself. "Oh Berit, why don't you take my garbage because that's what you are – trash."

"You guys stop bickering, that's what you are - The Bickersons," Philly snaps.

Several delightfully rude minutes later something catches my eye. Could it be? A lone slice left on the plate to shrivel in the summer evening heat?

As tempting as it is, we figure snatching the whole piece would be too noticeable. So we sample some slightly chewed crust. It's pretty good (good enough, in fact, that following night we indulge in a pizza of our own).

We mill around a little longer, forgetting the leftover slice for a moment, and when curiosity steers my eyes back to the lone pizza slice ... it is missing!

Frantically my eyes dart around to see where it's gone.

The plate is there, but the pizza is not. Finally my eyes settle on an American girl standing nearby. This is the first time I've seen here. She is friends with one of the girls that ordered the pizza and was therefore an heir to the remaining piece.

She has the pizza in her hand.

I think I watched her eat the whole thing. It was like a train wreck - I tried to look away but I couldn't.

And just like that, it was gone.

- Caitlyn Slivinski

Four million pilgrims

EVEN ON THIS RAINY DAY the town is full of people.

Only upon a closer look do you realize that the large group gathered under the portico of the building next to the basilica is made up of people partaking in a UNITALSI pilgrimage.

UNITALSI, one of the oldest Italian pilgrimage organizations was founded in 1903 with the aim of helping the ill visit religious locations of significance.

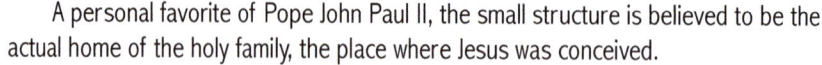

Within the Basilica of Loreto lies one of the most famous pilgrimage sites in Italy - The Holy House of Loreto.

A personal favorite of Pope John Paul II, the small structure is believed to be the actual home of the holy family, the place where Jesus was conceived.

Because of the mystical occurrences surrounding the House, Loreto is also considered to be a location for those hoping to recover from illnesses.

The Holy House of Loreto is partially famus for the myth behind the moving to its current location. In 1263 the Holy Land in the Middle East was taken over by Islam. It is then said that angels came in 1291 and flew the house to Dalmatia, now Croatia, where it was revealed to be the home of Mary.

Three years later angels moved it to what is now the town of Loreto.

The Holy House of Loreto consists of single room with an alter containing a Black Madonna statue. The ceiling is blue with gold stars. In 1469 the giant, ornate Basilica was built over the Holy House. The Basilica has since been renovated numerous times.

Today Loreto, which overlooks the sea, is one of the most visited pilgrimage sites in Europe, with an estimated 4 million visitors arriving each year.

- Berit Baugher

Actually worth the hike

IT IS PRACTICALLY impossible not to pull over.

From the road, the turquoise water and white sand beaches look more like a postcard than natural Italian scenery.

A long dusty path lined with a wooden fence winds down to the beach. The rock-free soft dirt may be too difficult for a pair of flip-flops. Bare feet provide more grip and stability to combat the steep descent.

Along the path there are various look out points with wooden benches providing the perfect opportunity to rest and snap photos. The only thing more daunting than walking down the path is the prospect of the steep return trip home.

Once you have reached beach level, there is one small restaurant that serves typical beach snacks along with various seafood dishes. The fresh seafood is prepared on a grill that can be seen from the tablecloth covered picnic tables that look out on the water.

Unlike the other public beaches in the region, Mezzavalle is more natural. Free from rows of umbrellas, identical snack shops, and the traffic of busy roads, the beach has a secluded serenity as if only a small Italian population is aware of its location or willing to make the trek to its waters.

The sand is fine and white except where the waves roll in, leaving a strip of smooth colorful round stones. Glistening with salty seawater their dazzling colors and smooth textures tempt beachcombers to fill empty pockets.

Walking back up the path after a day on the sand, beads of sweat from the physically demanding ascent drip onto ocean water-covered skin, marking clinging clothes with a film of white salt.

Once at the top, however, a feeling of accomplishment adds a new dimension of finding the beautiful beach below.

The pocket full of rocks, now dry and free from the sun's reflection are dull and rough, unimpressive out of their natural habitat.

Only another trip down to the beach can return the natural souvenirs to their brilliance.

- Philly Petronis

Mountains of possibilities

MAKING MY WAY down the beach I stop every few feet and lower myself to a squatting stance.

My eyes search the naturally rocky shore in hopes of spotting a small speck of green sea glass amongst the varying gray and cream-colored rocks. The crash of a wave pierces my ears and I instinctively jump up in avoidance of soaking the towel I have wrapped around my shoulders.

Before me is the great Adriatic Sea. The long stretch of beach I am walking on is only one of many lining the eastern shore of Italy. Unknown to most American travelers the Conero Riviera is a truly spectacular sight.

The crystal clear blue water goes out as far as I can see and the air is rich with the smell of salt. Restaurants line the beach and specialize in various seafood dishes. But here in Mezzavalle there is only one.

Behind the shore is Monte Conero and the surrounding mountains of the Le Marche region. It is possible to be in the country at a vineyard and then laying on the beach in less then 20 minutes.

The area supplies a host of activities including horseback riding, hiking, biking, various water sports and a plethora of small traditional medieval towns to visit.

The friendly demeanor of the local Italians vibrates throughout the resort towns and small villages and it is here on Italy's Adriatic coast that one can have a truly wonderful experience.

I drop the small rounded pieces of glass into the plastic bag I'm using to hold my collection and make my way back towards my friends.

- Berit Baugher

Sky high and loving it

THE ROAD TO THE top of Monte Petrano is a sidewinder - and a difficult one at that.

The curves are sharp and the incline is steep. Our little Lancia's engine screamed the whole way up.
Amazingly, along the road, there were bicyclists chugging up to the top where cool breezes are the ultimate reward.
There were hundreds of people relaxing in the cool air on the flat top of the mountain, one of the highest in the region. People played bocce, flew kites and ate picnics. A few people were harnessing the strong winds in huge kites that pulled them on skateboards and in little buggies.
The vast expanse of land is a doggie wonderland. The open fields are great places for pooches to run on blazing summer days.

- G. Miller

Everything and Nutella

COME TO NUMANA if you love the beach, beautiful sights and a night out on the town.

It doesn't hurt to be a dog-lover either.
There isn't a better place to spend your time (or money) than a place like Numana. Located in the Le Marche region just minutes from the Ancona airport, Numana offers enthusiastic travelers a chance to wine and dine at delicious (and affordable) Italian eateries and spend the night at luxurious or more reasonable hotels, depending on what suits you.

The Gigli Hotel is located right in Numana on a cliff overlooking the Adriatic Sea. The hotel offers its guests great food and isolation from the rest of the town, surrounded by trees that close it off and make it barely noticeable as you walk by. For those guests who prefer a more fast, upbeat nightlife, they are minutes away from the center of the town where there is dancing, music and several café bars. For more information, contact the Gigli hotel at 071 9330930 or email at info@giglihotels.com.

For those looking to pay less and still have a great stay, Hotel Giardino and Sorriso are more affordable. Both are located in Numana and are also just a short walk away from the town. For more information on both, call 1-800-434-6835 or check them out at hotels.com. You can also stay at a hotel in Sirolo, a town similar to Numana about one kilometer away.

Spending a day at the beach in Numana can only be described as relaxing. English-speaking travelers won't feel abandoned or alone while traveling in Numana, as many of the employees speak enough English to make sure you get your panini order just right, but not enough to make you feel like you're back in the States.

There are literally dozens of places to eat throughout the town but I have to recommend Al Pelozzo di Mare. The menu lists an array of food, but the restaurant's specialty is pizza, which tastes like little slices of heaven. The restaurant is located on a side street in Numana and offers outdoor seating, which is perfect on a warm summer night. The telephone number is 07117360133 and website is nemtudom@libero.it.

The Landmarks

The stores in Numana are also worth a visit. Ranging from exotic necklaces to Nutella in a jar, there is almost any souvenir being sold by friendly, helpful Italians. There is a outdoor market in the piazza during the evening, so while preparing to do some dancing, you can peruse the tables full of hand-made jewelry, scarves, T-shirts, mugs, bowls, personalized postcards, and sparkly pants.

Like most towns in Italy, Numana seems to be home for a lot of dogs. Good-looking dogs, heinous-looking dogs, short, fat, skinny, long, hairy and hairless dogs. You name it, Numana's got it. I've found that Italian culture embraces their pets more on an every-day basis. Sure, Americans love their dogs. But seeing a dog not on a leash or sitting with his owner at a café is rare if not unheard of here .

Numana is just another place to see how much Italians treasure their dogs.

- Ann Curran

Princess for a day?

THE MEDIEVAL FORTRESS, the "Rocca," is the highlight of the small town of Offagna.

For 3 euros you can tour the fortress that was built between 1452 and 1456.

Ducking under low doorways, walking along uneven dirt floors and climbing rickety stairs to the fortress' roof somehow has the ability to transport you back to medieval times.

Glass cases in various rooms throughout the castle contain medieval knight armor, knives, and rifles to further stimulate the fortress's historical importance as a means of defense.

From the top of the fortress there are beautiful views and a nice breeze. If you get a thrill by disturbing serenity, you can ring the big bronze bell cast in 1477 and engraved with the Ancona coat of arms. Offagna once protected the ancient port city from invaders from the west.

Cobblestone streets weave towards pizzerias, small markets and bakeries nestled inconspicuously behind ornate doorframes. The architecture of various churches and towers dating back to the fifteenth century are impressive and intact, making it feel like I was walking through a functioning museum.

From July 22 to July 29 Offagna hosts a medieval festival. A brochure promises that fire-eaters, minstrels, ladies and knights will be roaming the streets.

Our visit sparks enough interest to return, possibly dressed as princesses, to take part in the festivities.

- Philly Petronis

Tower leads to nude beach!

AT THE END OF A long, white gravel road, an old brick tower stands alone, fenced off and surrounded by trees that lean toward the adjacent Adriatic Sea. The path to the tower's entrance is full of overgrown bushes and weeds, and the whole facility appears to be neglected and unappreciated.

When it was built around 1808, the tower was a sentinel station for the nearby Fortina Napoleanica, a defensive structure erected by the Italian viceroy Eugenio Behauharnais. The role of the tower and the fort was to prevent the English Navy from approaching the Italian kingdom.

The imposing majestic building maintains its classic, orange-tiled roof but the tower appears to be unmanned now. It is a monument to a feudal past and its only current purpose is to provide a landmark for sun worshippers.

Just south of the tower are dozens of people laying on the white pebble beach, romping in the clear blue water or eating at the small outdoor café. Husbands and boyfriends rub suntan lotion on their already tan wives and girlfriends, many of whom are topless.

It is quiet but for the sounds of the splashing waves and the laughter of children. There are no screeching motorini noises like you hear everywhere else in Italy.

Around the bend, in a secluded alcove due south of the tower, there is an entirely different scene: a nudist beach. It is the most recent, remote beach that the naturalists have claimed their own even though naked sunbathing is prohibited by law in Italy.

"It is forbidden," says Marco Bravi, an Italian language and culture instructor from Camerano, "but often tolerated by police."

But only in this one place in the region. For example, nude bathing in Sirolo, a beach town 8 kilometers to the south, reportedly carries a 500 Euro (about $625) penalty.

To find the tolerated nudist beach, you must park your car at the dead end of the road to Portonovo and then walk 15 minutes through thick brush and over rocks toward the old, white stone Santa Maria di Portonovo church.

"You need good shoes," says Bravi.

When the trail ends, you have to climb over a rock wall using a rope left there just for that purpose.

Of course, you can also find the nudist beach by following the beach line.

Just look for the tower and head south.

- G. Miller

Home of the poet Leopardi

THE TOWER THAT STANDS in the heart of Recanati was built around 1160 to unify the three castles that made up the town.

The imposing tower is 36 meters tall and can be seen for miles around.

But Recanati is more famous as the home of one of Italy's most well-known poets, Giacomo Leopardi (1798-1837).

Leopardi, of whom a statue now stands in the main piazza, was born and raised in the southern side of town and there are plaques referencing his life's accomplishments and works around the small, walkable city.

You can visit Leopardi's palazzo which is now a library and museum open to the public.

The town is a major attraction for Italians and foreigners alike, mostly because of Leopardi but also because the city is on the pilgrimage path to Loreto.

When we were there, the city was flooded with tourists from Japan, Great Britain, Germany and elsewehere.

- G. Miller

Land of velvet beaches

THE OLD MEN RIDE BIKES through the center of the old town, talking on cell phones and staring at the pretty young ladies.

A popular seaside resort since the mid 1800's, Senigallia retains its charms as well as its famous "Velvet Beach," the 13 kilometers of sandy apron leading into the refreshing waters.

There is also great history to the city. Founded in the 4th century BC, the town became a prosperous merchant city because of its location. Even today, there are shops and boutiques all over the place.

At the heart of the city is the old Rocca Roveresca, the brick fort that once defended the city.

- G. Miller

Sparky watches the world

SPARKY LIKES TO WATCH the world go by from his perch on the window ledge of a fuit shop in the upper section of Sirolo.

He has quite a view.

On summer evenings, Sirolo is a popular spot for vacationing Italians and other Europeans. Sparky can see all the latest fashions being sported by the high-rolling crowd. There is often live music in the piazza just down the road from his shop. There are art exhibits across the street and a million gelato shops nearby.

The beautiful resort city at the southern base of Monte Conero was first inhabited by the Greeks, well before the Roman Empire came to the East coast of Italy.

Now the area is populated by sun-worshippers who appreciate the gentle breezes during hot summer nights.

- G. Miller

Jewel of the Conero Riviera

JUST STEPS FROM THE SEA, Sirolo is considered by many to be the "Jewel of the Conero Riviera."

The beautiful town is surrounded by steep cliffs overlooking long stretches of beach and white rocks covered in pinewood.

Upon entering the medieval town you will not fail to be greeted by Sparky, a local mutt. He sits on the windowsill of his owner's store, a fruit and vegetable market, eagerly awaiting the arrival of tourists and locals on their way to town.

The main piazza overlooks the sparkling green water of the Adriatic. On the other side of the piazza are shops and cafes. The center of the town sticks out over a cliff similar to the way a balcony juts off the side of a building.

At night the many cafes and gelaterias fill with people and the shops buzz with action.

Upon entering the piazza, directly to the left, one can find the Tourist Information Center. This is helpful if one is planning on staying in the area for a while. They have a range of brochures advertising local activities such as wine vineyards, horseback riding, water parks and theatres.

To the right of the Tourist Information Center is an art gallery, which I have yet to see open but which looks very promising. Through the window I am able to make out several attractive looking paintings of sunflowers, apparently based on the local scenery.

The center of the piazza is comprised of several small cafes. My favorite being L'Oasis Gelateria. Although I have not tried the ice cream I came one evening for drinks and was pleased with the location and service.

Across from the L'Oasis Gelateria sits one of the many local alimentare, the Italian version of a small grocery store. The store is underwhelming from the outside but upon entering it feels as though you are in a different world. The small shop is meticulously organized and appears to be maintained by a perfectionist.

The tiny refrigerated section is directly to your left when you walk in. It contains various packaged meats and cheeses. In the center of the store sits an assortment of brown wicker baskets filled to the brim with ripe tomatoes, vibrant red and yellow peppers and a variety of other fresh fruits and vegetables.

The store overflows with the smell of new produce and the slightly less appealing tinge of dirty sneakers. The source of the less attractive smell can be attributed to the cheese counter in the back of the store. Through the glass case a wide range of cheeses can be seen. From your traditional mozzarella to your feta and parmesan, it appears to all be there. The owners are friendly and were not the least bit taken aback that I leave without buying anything.

Along the main street there are several gelaterias to chose from; nevertheless there is clearly a favorite in my mind. The Gelateria Artigianale is your typical Italian ice cream parlor; however the cones are what make it truly stand out.

Most gelatarias, in my experience, offer the cake cone, which has a consistency similar to that of a piece of cardboard.

Gelateria Astigianole's waffle cones are freshly made and the taste attests to that. The shop's gelato flavors range from your average vanilla and chocolate to your more interesting pistachio and Nutella.

As always I opt for my traditional yogurt flavored gelato and rejoice in the option of having a waffle cone.

The small narrow streets branching off of the piazza have a variety of clothing and accessory shops ranging from your typical Italian sunglass shop to your quintessential Italian tobacharia.

The first store I enter is called Ceramica "Sirolese." The size of the shop is no larger than 20 by 20 feet. Crammed with small ceramic goods, the store appears overwhelming at first. Initially my eye is caught by the display being set up by the owner: sea horses, star fish, fish and shells hanging on a net over the front door. The ceramic creatures vary in size and the colors range from your typical sea blue to an iridescent moss green and a vibrant tangerine orange.

When assembled, the display is quite shocking and I am almost enticed to invest in my own net and collection of ceramic sea creatures.

Once out on the main street I pass an interesting looking store on my right. The door is wide open and an array of items can be seen displayed around the store. Tutto Arte is not your average store. It sells a wide variety of goods with a common element being the fact that they are all pieces of art.

There are various types of jewelry and pieces of furniture. The back wall is lined with paintings and small sculptural pieces. Initially I am drawn to a large crystal that can be hung from a cord and then worn as a necklace but at last minute I choose a small conch shell that is edged in silver. The bohemian artsy feel of the store is common in Italy and there always seems to be at least one store of its kind in every town.

Further down the main street I come across a longer side street, which leads me to a discount sunglass store. Every surface is covered in sunglasses and reading glasses for both men and women. The designers range from Escada to Calvin Klein. The store's air-conditioning provides me with a nice break from the heat.

Towards the end of the main street I come across a small pizza store, Rosticeria della Pizza al Taglio. The piazza served is traditional Italian pizza in that the crust is very thin; however this pizza parlor opts to serve their slices as triangles rather than your more traditional square.

At the end of the street and just outside of the town, I walk under a large stone archway. Here I come across the towns well known theatre "Cortesi." This theatre is also the box office box of the outdoor theatre "Alle Cave." Both theatres are infamous during the summer for their lyrical operas. "Alle Cave" is also known to be used as a discothèque late at night.

Further down the street I enter a residential section of Sirolo. The houses are large and the gate of the first house is adorned with tiles spelling out Villa Giulia. The large yellow building is hidden behind a fence. From what I can see it is clearly a beautiful old building surrounded by lush gardens.

Various villas continue to line the street, which eventually leads to the main road which will take you through Numana, another town, and then to a long stretch of beaches.

- Berit Baugher

White wine country

WHEN WE ARRIVED at the home of Sandro Finocchi, which also happens to be the family vineyard, his 86-year old father was sitting on the porch.

It was a hot summer day and the old man welcomed us, despite our not having an appointment. He immediately began talking to us, in Italian, of course.

Soon enough, he gave up trying to communicate with us and he called for his son, the operator of the winery.

Sandro walked us around the 8 hectare property in the heart of Verdicchio country and he talked about the production of his wine. His two daughters, Elena, 16, and Chiara, 11, run the bottling machine and they label the wine by hand. They joined us on our brief tour.

"I live upstairs, I work here," Sandro said with a laugh. "I don't leave too much!"

The small operation produces about 40,000 bottles per year, with much of the wine going to restaurants in Rome.

In the fermentation room, Sandro cleaned a few glasses and then poured white wine for us, straight from the cold steel tanks. It was fantastic.

After an hour or so, Sandro invited us to see the wine shop he is building nearby in the ancient city of Staffolo. The shop is a labyrinth of rooms and walkways that are built right into the old castle walls. He showed us tunnels that lead to other people's homes and shops.

Deeper in the city is a museum dedicated to the Verdicchio wine that is produced nearly everywhere here.

- G. Miller

The Lessons
The dos and don'ts of Le Marche

- Sunsets and fisherman, tourists and la dolce vita
- ...end on the first
- Get clean on the cheap
- Who is the blonde chick?
- Have a drink and watch the kids play
- Chillin' in Italia
- Get with the stick
- Thanks to the NY Post
- Please don't touch the bananas
- And horse meat
- Relax. Stay a while.
- I know I screwed up but I want my stuff!
- Yellow is the new black
- The ultimate wine tour
- Healing shawls keep tourists warm
- The greatest mistake ever made
- Get a room with a view
- How to sun for free
- Dance like no one is watching
- Even the warriors were bored
- Wine and walking in a truly pleasant place
- We're riding on the escalator of life
- Dinner straight from the Sea
- Beauty in the breakdown
- Stamp your ticket
- WHY TRAVEL?

La dolce vita

WHILE THERE IS AN ABUNDANCE of amazing places to see and exciting things to do in Le Marche, one of the most simple, enjoyable things to do here is watch the sunset.

From Portonovo you can watch the sun drop below the mountains near Ancona, casting an orange glow across the Eastern horizon of the Adriatic Sea.

By the time the sun sets, the beaches have cleared out, the parking attendants have gone for the day and the gentlemen in Speedos have retreated (for the most part). In Portonovo, you can enjoy the silence and natural beauty.

And it is free.

- G. Miller

The Lessons

Who's on the first?

CONSCIOUS OF MY FELLOW travelers low tolerance for museums and recognizing the potential for an aggressive backlash, I decide to make a solitary trip to Ancona to visit the Archeology Museum.

After being highly disappointed by the amphitheater ruins which are overgrown with weeds and fenced off from the public, I hope to find some English explanations of the random rock formations around the city's historic section. I want to know why they deserve to be preserved behind metal barriers.

I pay 2 euros to enter (it's 4 euro if you're over 25) the museum and I receive directions to guide me through. In broken English, a museum employee explains that I must skip the first floor and begin on the second floor, proceed to the third floor, and end on the first floor.

Before letting me go, he asks if I understand and then repeats the directions until he accepts my nodding head.

As I begin to navigate my tour, it becomes clear that the museum's exhibition rooms are as confusing as the museum's layout.

With no real direction I wander through 90-degree rooms with creaky floors, searching for something to spark my interest.

Most of the artifacts are from the Paleolithic period to the Middle Ages and they all look the same to me. My ignorance is magnified by the fact that only Italian explanations accompany the pieces.

I begin to feel like a maze-trapped rat searching for cheese when I realize I have to go to the bathroom. Semi-enjoyable aimless wandering is replaced by a desperate race to escape.

Rooms have multiple doorways. Strategically placed fire extinguishers or ropes block possible exits. Promising outlets turn out to be dead ends in little hot rooms.

My pending claustrophobia and failure to find a bathroom are making me miserable but I feel obligated to continue. If I start towards an exit, a random museum employee pops up to guide me back to the exhibit.

"Grazie," I say smiling sheepishly, pretending that I am merely disoriented, not undertaking a master breakout scheme.

I pause in front of some jewelry to feign some interest. These people devote their lives to these old rocks and artifacts; I can't be a completely ignorant American.

I am flooded with relief when I reach the main stairwell, relief that I am free at last and relief that I didn't force my friends to join me.

Now if I could only find the bathroom!

- Philly Petronis

Get clean on the cheap

NO SHOWER? NO PROBLEM!

There's no reason to stay sand-covered and salt-flavored after a day at the beach, and we learned just how easy it is to stay clean.

- Ann Curran

Even without the traditional shower curtain.

We found ourselves in a dilemma when our money spending started to exceed our money savings. It was only after a day of swimming in the Adriatic near Fano and allowing sand to accumulate all over our bodies did we realize that a decent hotel room was out of the question.

That's when Philly came to a mind-blowing epiphany: bathe in the Cagli waterfall where we love to swim. It's free, it's clean, and it's really the only option we had. Sure, the water was a little cold and there were tiny minnows brushing up against our legs while we shaved them. But once we got past these minor details — as well as the onlookers stares, points and laughter - we were as good as clean.

What better way can you freshen up (and in the process help preserve the environment) than bathing and washing in a natural body of water?

And unless you're planning on moving to the Sahara, you're never more than a few minutes away from a nice, clean shower.

Especially here in the mountainous Le Marche region.

Andiamo Le Marche – American Odyssey through Authentic Italy

We practice what we preach...

Caitlyn, Philly, Annie and I return to Cagli, our home for a month last summer, to watch the World Cup championship game between Italy and France.

We are drained from spending the day in Fano but we are anxious.

With no plan other than showing up, we arrive in the piazza still dirty from a day at Fano's beach. We have nothing more than a change of clothes and our sandy beach towels. Not seeing anyone we know we decide to resort to our back-up plan and head north toward the waterfalls, one of Cagli's best-known spots for hot summer days.

The waterfalls are located slightly outside of town but easily within walking distance. The small path leading down the hill, however, is steep and the slightest misstep could lead to a very serious injury.

Having said that, we make our way down, excited at the prospect of returning as well as eager to wash the salt from the ocean off of our bodies. The path is small and winds down the side of the mountain, ending at a rickety (but recently added) bridge.

After the bridge, we hop down to a collection of large rocks. We scale our way down the final rock only to be presented with a 15-foot drop.

This is the tricky part: I drop my bags and shoes down the drop and then proceed to slowly climb down, blindly placing my foot on small pieces of rock that jut out of the larger wall

Happy to reach the bottom I help bring down more bags as everyone else makes there way down.

Philly grabs her stolen bar of soap from the previous night's hotel, we climb over the rocks into the freezing cold mountain water and we proceed to bath.

Less than an hour later we emerge from the tall mountain weeds clean and in a fresh change of clothes, eager and happy to watch Italy humble the France.

- Berit Baugher

Who's that girl?

EDITOR'S NOTE: This entry comes to us from Alyssa Porambo, a blonde member of the 2006 Cagli Project.

EVER SINCE I WAS FIVE, I have had blonde hair. Long, straight golden locks have been my trademark look for so long that sometimes I am unaware of my dominant physical attribute. Many people in the States have blonde hair, and so I usually slip into the crowd as just another flaxen girl.

In the small town of Cagli, Italy, on the other hand, it is a completely different story.

I have never been so aware of my blondeness since staying in Cagli for one month.

Cagli is composed almost entirely of brunettes.

As I walked through the streets of the old town the day I arrived, I was much too excited to notice anything besides the beautiful stone buildings and the charm of the people. After a few days, however, I began to notice how few blondes I saw strolling around the piazza.

Eventually, I push back the questions I have about blondes in Cagli, thinking they are all in my head. Still, at the halfway mark of my stay in Italy, I had yet to meet a blonde Cagliese.

Are Italians from this region not naturally blonde? Why had I not seen a woman even with bright blonde highlights? Is being blonde not popular? It did not seem that way to me because every time I went out with my friends, the Italian men would ask to have their picture taken with me. Some of them would just stare at my hair in awe, and some would even come up to me and begin stroking my hair, reminding me of a childhood occurrence.

Picture this: I am sitting on a train in Florence with my parents and my younger brother. I am eight years old. An older Italian woman walks in my direction, stops, and stares at my head. She begins moving slowly towards me and finally, there she is, standing in front of me.

Unsure of what to do, I look to my mom for some guidance but she is just as confused as I am. Suddenly, I feel a hand on my head, moving back and forth. It is at this moment I realize that the woman is stroking my hair, intensely examining it. She's smiling at me, repeating the phrase "Che bella! Che bella!" over and over.

Soon, everyone in the train is staring in our general direction, looking for the source of great joy for this woman. She then bent down, pinched my cheeks, and said, "Bella Americana!"

Then she just walked away, leaving a very confused eight-year-old girl to wonder what the heck just happened.

My family had moved to Germany to live for three years when I was seven years old. Throughout our time in Europe, we traveled extensively: France, Austria, Switzerland, the Czech Republic, Poland, Germany and Italy. Every new place we went, the natives had different reactions to my hair color.

In Austria, for instance, I was never looked at as different or strange; I blended into the crowd nicely. In France, I was clearly American, but there was no overwhelming reaction to my appearance.

The Italian people, however, opened my eyes to the great distinction between blonde and brunette. The incident on the train was my first encounter with a reaction of astonishment to my hair color but it was not the last.

We traveled to Italy three times while living in Germany, and every time we went, I would be pointed at, smiled at, and gawked at. As a 10-year-old walking the streets of Rome with my mom, an old woman grabbed my hand and pulled me down so she could touch my hair.

"What the heck is it with these Italians and loving blonde Americans?" I would wonder to myself every time I would be pointed at, stared at.

As a 17-year-old, I returned to Italy with a group of friends. My friend Kelsey and I were the only two blonde girls on the trip. Similar to my experiences as a child, we received a multitude of looks from Italians, but this time, it was not from cute Italian grandmothers.

This time, they came from Italian men, believing that being blonde had a much different connotation than "Hi, I'm American, come and pet my head, please."

We would not even have to open our mouths and speak English for them to realize we were American, flock over and begin talking to us in Italian.

So when I found out I was returning to Italy in the summer of 2006, I prepared myself for the worst. I expected men to flock to me, women to point at me, and children to look at me like I had three heads.

And boy was I right.

Shouts of, "Americana! Americana!" could be heard throughout the main piazza in Cagli the moment I stepped off that bus. And they have continued throughout my time here.

It is as if these people have not seen a blonde woman in their lives! Is it really that rare to see a blonde in this town? Italian magazines and Italian television are both saturated with blonde women. Is it not the same to see a blonde woman in a picture as to see one in real life?

When I finally meet a blonde woman in Cagli, I am so excited! But then I learn that she is originally from Bulgaria and moved to Cagli when she got married.

"There are no blondes in Cagli," she says as she shakes her head. "I am convinced!"

Suddenly, it became my mission to find at least one blonde native Cagliese before I returned to the States. There has to be at least one blonde Italian roaming around here somewhere!

However, my quest turns out to be much more difficult than I had expected. Every baby, teenager, and woman I came across ss brunette. Even when I go to the local grocery store, Sidis, I can find no hair care products for blondes. As I hopefully scan the shelves for any sign of blonde life in Cagli, I conclude that it is nowhere to be found.

When I spoke to one of the local hairdressers about blondes, Matteo Susini, he informed me of the reasons why there is a great lack of flaxen girls in this region of Italy.

"Most of the blondes come from northern, not Central Italy," he says. "It is very rare to see a natural blonde walking through the streets of Cagli because most people from this region are dark haired."

"Also, women here do not want to be dyed blonde because it takes too much maintenance," Matteo, a blonde, continues. "Blonde highlights are more popular because of the minimal upkeep."

Finally, armed with the reasons why there are few blonde women in the town of Cagli, I take to the ancient streets holding my head up high.

I am one of very few in this town who dares to sport light locks and darn it, I will embrace it.

Being blonde in a brunette city was strange for me at first, but I now embrace my ability to make a sad man happy with a flick of my neck, the toss of my hair and a smile on my face.

I am an American. I am a blonde. And I am so proud.

- Alyssa Porambo

Have a drink with the kids?

ONLY IN EUROPE would a bar be built to accompany a public playground.

At first, Bar Summer Time seems like a perfect combination. A parent can sit back and relax with a couple cocktails as the screaming and running hyperactive children slowly become tolerable.

Then I think about this in an American context and realize that this could probably classify a parent as an alcoholic, hence the reason I'm not ready for children.

The shack style bar that serves ice cream, snacks and drinks has become a popular hangout for us Americans after our Monday night dinners. The TV, foosball and playground complete with a mini-roller rink, slides and swings provide more forms of amusement than the typical billiard table or jukebox.

However, I recommend some supervision if you decide to play after drinking.

It isn't until mid-flight, after jumping about ten feet off my swing, that I realize another reason that playgrounds and drinking don't mix in America.

- Philly Petronis

Chillin' in Italia

ITALY IS KNOWN for its olive oil, wine and pasta but on hot summer days, gelato is what I crave.

Gelato is the Italian word for ice cream. But anyone who has tried freshly made gelato can attest to the fact that it is better than Hagan-Daz, Baskin Robins or TCBY any day.

The cold, slippery-smooth texture is excellent whether sitting in a cup or atop a cone. Most importantly you can find numerous gelaterias or cafés with gelato at any point in time while in Italy.

Gelato differs from American style ice-cream in that the taste is denser. It's made with less air but at the same time, the gelato is slightly less filling. Gelato is considered to be healthier than ice cream because the ingredients consist of less butterfat and more natural components such as fruit, coco, and in some cases even olive oil. Gelato is made daily, while ice cream can contain chemicals preservatives that allow it to be stored in the freezer for months.

L'Altro Mondo located just feet from the piazza in Camerano has what I consider to be an excellent assortment of gelato flavors. Their options range from your typical vanilla and chocolate to Nutella, a gelato version of the popular chocolate-hazelnut spread, and Bacio, a take on one of Italy's most famous candies.

My personal favorite is the yogurt flavor while my friend Annie prefers café and chocolate mixed together.
Regardless of what you chose, its hard to go wrong.

- Berit Baugher

Stick shift saga

IF THERE'S ONE THING I've learned from being abroad for an elongated period of time, it's this: you have to know how to drive a stick shift.

After a fun day of horseback riding, we were hot, famished, cranky and tired.
We desperately wanted to cool off, eat, sleep and not talk. George, our chaperone and designated driver (meaning the only one among us who knows how to drive a stick-shift), sensed our moods.
Cranking the AC and driving a little faster than usual, we began to leave the farm.
Just as we were approaching the exit, we felt the car struggling against the rough terrain and steep slope of a gravel-road hill. We were so close to the top and then suddenly the car was backpedaling down the hill.
"This is what my horse kept doing," I said in an attempt to lighten the mood.
The car clearly needed more momentum to successfully climb over the hill.
As George attempted to maneuver the stubborn car, Chas - in shotgun - encouraged George's driving. Chas' cool attitude kept the rest of us somewhat calm. Berit and Caitlyn had more trouble relaxing than Philly and me, especially when the car began to tip.

"That's it!" Berit exclaimed from the backseat. "Let me out!"
With Chas acting a traffic controller, Berit hiding in the bushes and Caitlyn laughing and taking pictures, George, Philly and I faced the hill (from inside the tilted car) and trudged upward.
Luckily for us, it only took one more try for George to make the little Lancia climb up the hill.
One try for George would have equaled eight or nine attempts for any of the non-experienced stick shift drivers.
If not more. Thank heaven for small favors.
But it was really then, at that moment, did I realize how necessary it was for a person to be able to drive using a stick shift while cruising around the hilly terrain of the Le Marche region.

We all let out a celebratory hurrah (and also sighs of relief) when we were back on track and over this stubborn hill. Thanks to George, we were on our way.
While it's easiest to learn when you're first learning to drive, it's never too late to become familiar with a stick shift. And I suggest you realize this before traveling abroad for a month.

- Ann Curran

The Horse with no name

LEO - YOUR HOROSCOPE FOR JULY 13, 2006:

"It is important that you make an effort to overcome your fears today, because if you don't you will be held back from doing something that could have been a lot of fun. The choice is simple: live up to your true potential or look back a few years from now and lament what might have been. You can make your dreams come true."

After reading my horoscope from the New York Post, I knew I had to go horseback riding even though I didn't really want to.

I didn't have a choice.

It's not that I'm scared of horses. It's not like I survived some terrible, traumatic fall off a bucking horse and broke my nose and the chances of me ever riding again were slim to non-existent.

The truth is, I'd never been on a horse.

But to say that I was "thrilled" to go horseback riding would be a bit of a stretch.

Actually, it would be a flat-out lie. But more than I hate sitting on wild, unpredictable animals, I hate not forcing myself to try something new. And so, on a miserably hot and humid Thursday afternoon, we set out for the farm to face my fears.

When we arrived at Il Corbezzolo, I was not entirely surprised by what I saw. There were a dozen or so horses roaming around a fenced-in pen. Horses the color of midnight, dirt, and yogurt gelato, and some with a perfect blend of all three.

Eric, the man who seemed to be in charge, walked toward me with sweat dripping down his face and a cigarette hanging out his mouth. With a thick leather strap, he pulled a magnificent looking white creature behind him. He pointed directly to me, and then to the horse.

With no words exchanged, I understood. This horse was mine.

Or I was the horse's.

I stepped one foot into the stirrup and threw my body over the horse (which I was told had no name), hoping my weight would not crush him. He barely moved. I stroked his pasty white mane and made clicking noises near his writhing ears.

So far, I wasn't freaking out. In fact, I felt calm as I sat perched on the horse, almost eager to break free from the enclosed pen and go up the mountain.

My horse seemed to sense that I trusted him and he obeyed nearly all of my commands via tugging and loosening the reins. The only times he veered off course were to munch on some green stalks along the side of the trail.

And even though Eric didn't speak English, I felt safe and comfortable while he smoked cigarettes and chatted on his cell phone, leading the way through the tall stalks of grass and eventually up a steep, thorn-filled hill while the rest of us obediently followed.

When we first approached the hill, I became nervous. I had remained relatively calm and was even somewhat enjoying myself up until that point. My horse proved to be sweet natured and calm but I wasn't sure if I could trust him with a mountain.

I was instructed to lean forward and allow the horse to plow through the rugged terrain. With each stride the horse made, I got more and more used to feeling like I was going to slide right off.

When we reached the top, the horse and I breathed in the fresh air. The view was breathtaking - the city on the hill, the bright sunlight on the green mountains and the pale blue sky.

The hard part was over. Now we both could relax.

Even though my fears almost prevented me from going, I'd encourage anyone to trudge through their own reservations.

If you don't you will be held back from doing something that could have been a lot of fun.

I don't know whether to thank Eric, the sweet-natured cream-colored horse or the writers at the New York Post for making me go through with riding but I am definitely happy that I did.

- Ann Curran

Grocery shopping rules

"ITALIAN WOMEN TYPICALLY go to the market everyday to buy fresh fruits and vegetables," explains our Italian teacher here in Camerano.

This must be why we Americans get stared at when we go to the market and stock up like we are preparing for a blizzard. Needless to say, buying groceries in an Italian supermarket is different from food shopping in the United States.

At home you just go into the store, grab a peach, for example, maybe squeeze it a few times to make sure it is ripe, and then toss it into a plastic bag.

Here, try to grab your peach and you get yelled at by the cashier whose arms are flailing like she's flagging a cab (and not getting one).

You soon realize that in Italy, you point to the produce of your choice and the grocery store workers retrieve it for you.

They don't want your dirty hands touching another customer's potential purchase.

At some stores, it is up to you to select your peach and take it to a scale in the produce section but even then there are restrictions. First, you are supposed to wear disposable plastic gloves supplied by the store. Second, you are supposed to weigh your own food and determine the price. You match the button on the scale with the fruit or veggie you are weighing.

The machine tallies your price and prints out a sticker with the proper amount plus a barcode. Slap that sticker on your fruit-filled plastic bag and you're ready to check out.

If you don't print up the sticker, it's quite the nuisance for the cashier to walk all the way back through the store and do it for you.

Plus you feel like a foreign idiot.

- Caitlyn Slivinski

... and horse meat

The city of Cantiano, nestled in the Appennine mountains, is rather well known for a city of 2,500 people.

First, there is a museum dedicated to the old Roman highway - the Via Flaminia - which runs through the city. In the area, there are numerous remains of the original road - large stone blocks and impressive, still-functioning bridges.

Second, there is a geological museum with a dinosaur named Ugo. Apparently, thousands upon thousands of years ago, the region was a non-Disney Jurassic Park.

Thirdly, on Good Friday every year, thousands of people come to Cantiano to watch the Passion Play which represents the condemnation, crucifixion and resurrection of Jesus Christ.

And finally, the people of Cantiano eat horse meat.

Yes, horse meat.

In the center of town, at the base of the hill where the remains of the old castle still stand, there are two meat butchers who both specialize in horse meat. And there are horse farms all around in the surrounding cuntryside.

Horse meat, apparently, isn't widely popular here but eating horse meat in Italy doesn't draw the same reaction as it would in America.

Give it a taste!

- G. Miller

Relax. Stay a while.

FOR LUNCH WE EAT mouth-watering spaghetti and drink white wine at a friendly restaurant on the beach while chatting about family, relationships and our trip so far.

Afterwards, we spend a stressful day sunbathing and collecting stones on the beaches of Mezzavalle.
Then in Castelfidardo, I enjoy a refreshing cone of café gelato.
Later at the same cafe, I watch in a combination of awe, amusement and astonishment as an elderly man argues and eventually scolds the waiter who has failed to fill his wine glass to the absolute brim.
Keep in mind that it is 1:30 in the afternoon on an otherwise insignificant Tuesday.
These are just a few examples of how life really slows down when you leave fast-paced American culture and enter Italian life.
Americans are notorious for despising anything slow. We cringe at the thought of a frozen computer screen and think the DMV could actually be the gateway to Hell.
You must realize before traveling to a place like Italy that life slows down.
When you go out to eat, dinner can take as long as three hours or more. There are no doggie bags. It is considered rude to rush your meal. Most stores outside of the larger Italian cities actually close between the hours of one and four PM so the Italians can leisurely stroll home and enjoy pausa, nap time.

Don't get me wrong. I love the way New York City literally seems to move. I love how fast I can get my French Vanilla ice coffee from Dunkin Donuts every morning. And I love how I don't have to stick around until I've sucked the entire thing down. I love asking for the check even before I've eaten the last bite, just to make sure I'm continuously on the go.

But it doesn't hurt anyone or anything to enjoy a glass of wine in the middle of the afternoon and know that this is not frowned upon.

In Italy, your presence will never be hurried out.

- Ann Curran

Survive Italy without luggage

IT WASN'T UNTIL I WAS sailing 40,000 feet high in the air - somewhere between Switzerland and Germany - that I realized that my two checked bags probably wouldn't be joining me in Ancona, my final destination.

I became aware of this dismal truth when I happened to notice my baggage tickets listed Zurich and Munich as arrivals with absolutely no mention of Ancona.

The flight attendant explained the simple solution: find my bags in the baggage claim and re-check them. Easy. The only problem was when my flight from Zurich landed and when my flight to Ancona left -10:15 AM and 10:45 AM respectively.

Surprisingly, my usual tweak of a self (I'm a spaz) remained calm. It is uncertain whether I can credit this to the several deep breaths I took, the fact that I was too delusional to fully comprehend what was going on (I hadn't slept for nearly twenty hours) or the painful truth that there was no one to blame but myself for not double-checking the destination of my own beloved bags. Somehow, I managed a friendly chat with the young girl sitting next to me for the remaining fifty minutes of the flight and I (briefly) forgot about my lost luggage.

For the next four days, I would be forced to do the unthinkable - the worst nightmare for a closet girly-girl: wear other people's T-shirts.

Yes, for the next four days (days I seemed to be photographed more often than Paris Hilton), I alternated between a navy Michigan tee and another that reads, "Czech Me Out," obnoxiously across the chest. While I was thankful my friends were generous with their clothes (I never once judged their taste), I also understandably wanted my own stuff.

Despite the twice-a-day showers and constant perfume spraying, I never felt rid of the sticky, overly-used stench that one acquires while traveling without a clean change into their own ratty T-shirt and mesh shorts. And so I was reluctantly forced to live a painful ninety-eight hours in this condition.

I knew I wouldn't live this way forever. I knew my bags and I would eventually be reunited and our embrace would be sweet and loving. I also knew that in the scheme of things, my ordeal was petty and my view on the whole thing was ridiculously absurd and juvenile.

I knew all these things, and yet they made no difference. I wanted my bags, and I wanted them now.

Anyone who has ever lost a bag while traveling can relate; it is those who lack the experience who simply don't get how miserable it truly is.

So while it was a painful (and smelly) four days, it was also four days that helped me form an unbreakable bond with anyone else who has ever lost their luggage.

- Ann Curran

Yellow is the new black

THE TREND FOR men is yellow pants.

I've seen a lot of men, usually older, wearing pants the color of a ripe banana. It's not like the workman's neon pants. And they aren't pastel. They are rather some sort of a sun weathered yellow.

There are some variations. You might find yellow shorts instead of long pants. And some of the pants (and shorts) are more of an orange hue.

What kind of shirts might match the aforementioned fashion? The answer appears to be: anything. I've seen blue, red, striped, button-down and sports jerseys.

Sitting in the shade, wearing a lightweight dress and flip-flops, I'm sweating. There's no getting around today's heat.

I wonder if the yellow pants make men cooler?

- Caitlyn Slivinski

The ultimate wine tour

KEES DEKKER SIPPED a glass of Sassi Neri, a Rosso Conero wine, in the cantina of the La Terrazza vineyard and pronounced, "You don't drink this wine because it's just wine."

I nodded, not really knowing if I could fully appreciate the subtle differences in flavor. Visiting this famed vineyard that claimed connections to Bob Dylan, for me, meant drinking free wine in a chilled environment on a blazing summer day, plus the opportunity to learn a little about life in Italy.

Dekker, a Dutchman, savored the dry, fruity taste, paused and then declared, "This is a serious wine; it has complexity."

He and his wife had been vacationing in Le Marche every summer for the past four years and they were in the process of buying a second home here. They had initially looked in Tuscany and Umbria but they found that Le Marche was cheaper, less crowded with foreigners and far more diverse than anywhere else they had been.

"Italians say that Le Marche is Italy in one region," Dekker noted. "You have the sea, the mountains, all four seasons."

Like the wine, there is complexity in the region.

•

Le Marche begins at the Adriatic Sea, develops into gentle, rolling hills and ends in the massive, mile high Apennine Mountains.

As the terrain subtly evolves from sea level to foothills to high ground, there are minor disparities in people's attitudes and slight differences in cultures.

Residents of hilltop towns separated by only a few miles have different dialects and opposing outlooks on life. The special delicacy of one town may be unavailable in the next town down the road. The modest style of one city, while not necessarily noticeable to outsiders, may be different from the slightly less modest style of the next.

And that's the way they like things there.

"In America, things are black or white — things are good or bad," said Carlo Cleri, a representative of the Slow Foods movement branch in the medieval city of Cagli. "We like variety, difference. There is a lot of range between white and black."

Wine is a prime example: there are more than 250 government sanctioned varieties of wine produced in Italy, a country smaller than California where there are fewer than 30 varieties.

In Le Marche alone, there are 12 types of wine that are created here and nowhere else in the world. Each wine, labeled "D.O.C." (denominazione d'origine controllata, meaning wine of controlled origin), has its own characteristics that vary, if only slightly, from other wines produced in the region.

You could spend years exploring the hundreds of vineyards that exist in Le Marche, from worldwide production facilities to mom and pop farms. And whether or not you can savor the difference between a full-bodied Rosso Conero and an ethereal Rosso Piceno, touring wineries is a great way to experience the differences in our cultures, as well as the differences in theirs.

•

"You're walking on wine," Gianluca Garofoli said with a laugh as we entered the original fermentation room of his family's vineyard near the holy city of Loreto.

The English-speaking, 25-year old Gianluca explained that below the concrete floor at our feet, in two giant concrete tanks, were thousands of liters of Rosso Conero, the cherry-smelling red wine that is only produced in the area surrounding Monte Conero.

The old cellar - ripe with the aroma of sweet wine - was built in 1901 and is still used today even though the Garofoli family has completely modernized their facilities. Wine is also aged in huge, 900 liter wooden barrels as well as in steel tanks. In the basement of the adjacent building are 700 French barrels used to mature wine at 225 liters per barrel.

"Each generation has built this business, step by step," said Gianluca, whose grandfather's grandfather started the vineyard in 1871 along the pilgrimage path to Loreto, where the original home of the Virgin Mary has been for around 800 years.

Garofoli, a mid-sized winery with 1,400 acres of grape fields, now distributes 2.2 million bottles around the world annually.

The affable Gianluca, a Red Sox-loving baseball fanatic and heir to the family business, explained that the Garofoli family was among the first vintners to put wine in bottles - rather than jugs - in the latter half of the 19th century. In the 1950's, they were among the first in Italy to have a fully automated bottling plant.

"We totally changed the distribution of wine in Italy," he said.

Gianluca eagerly walked us around the state-of-the-art bottling plant where 5 workers watched machines package wine at 5,000 bottles per hour.

Then he offered us wine.

"And now we drink?" he asked.

So we sat down for a few hours, sampled several bottles of Garofoli reds and whites and we talked to Gianluca, the left fielder for the local squad, about life in Le Marche.

"I don't know if I love the Marche region but Monte Conero is beautiful," he said as he continued filling our glasses. "Everyone knows it around the world. This is a very good region to live."

Actually, Monte Conero and the Le Marche region remain rather unknown, especially in comparison to great Italian destinations like Rome, Venice and the heavily trafficked Tuscan region.

But Le Marche, due east of Tuscany, is a veritable treasure trove of charming medieval hill towns, pristine beaches and stunning vistas.

On a random drive, you can find vast fields of radiant, yellow sunflowers, ancient castles perched high upon mountaintops and charming little villages full of cafes and friendly people who don't speak a lick of English.

When we arrived unannounced on a scorching summer Sunday afternoon, Sandro Finocchi's 86-year old father was sitting in the shade on the porch of the modest family home, a handful of tiny, lazy kittens sprawled at his feet.

He immediately began talking to us in Italian as though we were old friends.

I had been in Italy for more than a month at that point, teaching in a journalism program for American college students, so my language skills were almost acceptable.

Still, I could barely understand the lively old man. He seemed to be rambling on and on in a local dialect about being a prisoner of war in a Turkish camp during World War II.

Finally, he called for his son, the operator of the Azienda Agricola Finocchi vineyard.

Sandro Finocchi, clad in brown sandals, a black tank top and shorts, approached us with a smile and offered to give us a tour of his 20-acre property even though he was in the middle of eating lunch. His 16-year old daughter Elena acted as our translator.

"I live upstairs and I work here," Finocchi said. "I don't leave too much!"

We walked down a gentle sloping hill that was thick with grape vines and olive trees. Finocchi explained that the land had been in his family for generations but he began producing and selling wine in the mid 1980's. He pulled a small, rubbery branch off of a tree and showed us how he uses the twigs to bind vines to fencing.

"Everything is organic," he said. "We only use a minimal amount of chemicals to keep away parasites."

He produces about 40,000 bottles per year, mostly the crisp, white Verdicchio dei Castelli di Jesi, with much of the wine going to restaurants in Rome. And it is completely a family operation – Finocchi and his two daughters gather the grapes, bottle the wine, place labels on them and then box the final products.

The Lessons

Back at his home/factory, Finocchi cleaned a few glasses and poured us white wine straight from a stainless steel tank. "It's too cold," he said. "But that's good for a hot day like today."

Le Marche's verdicchio wines were popular in the years following World War II and their distinctive hourglass-shaped bottles became symbols of Italian restaurants around the world. As competition for sales increased, wine makers began lowering the quality of the product in order to lower the price.

That caused a backlash and the virtual end of verdicchio sales.

Over the past 20 years or so, Italian verdicchios have made a strong comeback. Some of the whites can now be aged for up to ten years, similar to high quality reds.

The fresh, white Bianchello del Metauro wine from the Guerrieri vineyard tastes like Le Marche. You can smell the dry farmland in the glass and you can almost taste the sea air that wafts over the fields.

The grapes are grown in the Metauro River valley, a few kilometers inland from the Adriatic Sea, on 500 acres of land that has been cultivated by the Guerrieri family for more than 200 years.

The grape variety, however, is much older and carries a sense of pride for the locals: legend has it, Luca Guerrieri told us, that the Bianchello del Metauro saved the Roman Empire.

The great Carthaginian general Hannibal had already taken much of Southern Italy when his brother, the commander Hasdrubal, began advancing upon Rome from the north.

On a hot summer night in 207 BC, Hasdrubal's troops made camp along the Metauro River and found a farmer with vast reserves of Bianchello del Metauro wine. The Carthaginian army reportedly drank gallons upon gallons of the refreshing drink and when the Roman legions attacked in the morning, the Carthaginians were either too drunk or hung over to survive.

Or so the story goes.

Of course, nearly all Italian wines are created with American roots grafted onto their vines.

A parasite, phylloxera, caught a ride to France from the U.S. in the 1860's and, within 25 years, wiped out most of the European vineyards. The solution to the almost-catastrophic event was to create hybrid plants which are still used today.

Some of the grapes produced in the region, like the LaCrima di Morro D'Alba, have retained their ancient flavors.

"LaCrima grapes are a special type of grape," said Carlo Cleri, 35, the Slow Foods proponent. "It's traditional, it has the flavor of old wines."

We had spent the afternoon touring the factory of the Stefano Mancinelli winery, with Stefano's parents, Fabio and Luisa, as our tour guides. The factory, which specializes in the LaCrima, wasn't much to look at but the family couldn't have been nicer to us. They sliced a blackberry pie and invited us to sit and taste their wines. The more questions we asked about them and their rose and violet-scented wine, the more they kept giving us stuff — books, pictures, wine labels.

Fabio Mancinelli began making wine about 50 years ago just for the love of doing so. He grew his own grapes on the hills near the castle-like city of Morro D'Alba. His passion became his son's business and now they are among the few farms that are allowed to grow the rustic-flavored grapes that can be given the name of LaCrima di Morro D'Alba.

"To me, this is the best wine," Cleri said. "It is a wine I usually open with a girl."

We visited the Capinera Winery, owned by a pair of BMW-driving brothers who are both architectural engineers in Rome. Paolo Capinera speaks a little English. Fabrizio is a sommelier. They started making wine on 18 acres of old family land near Morrovalle about ten years ago.

The brothers were excited to entertain us but they were also in a rush to go home to Rome, a three-hour drive away. They poured copious amounts of wine for us but rushed our tasting. It made our drive home pretty exciting.

Another day we visited the tourist friendly Conte Leopardi winery in Numana where the owner handed visitors glasses of wine as soon as they entered the shop.

An employee at the Moroder vineyard in Ancona escorted us through the cellar but never offered us wine. So we left.

At the Vicari vineyard in Morro D'Alba, locals were filling up large, 5-gallon jugs with LaCrima.

Silvano Strologo showed us huge, 27-liter bottles of his Rosso Conero at the Strologo vineyard in Camerano.

"I recently sold 3 bottles to someone in Germany," he laughed.

"Of course, Tuscany is always first," said Laura Baldinelli, an English-speaking export assistant at the Umani Ronchi winery in Osimo. "But Le Marche is very popular now as well."

Baldinelli spoke to us inside the 58 degree cellar that is designed to look like the inside a mine.

"Here, there are not diamonds but our top wines," she said.

The moist, dim room that was as stylish as a nightclub contained 500 French barrels containing roughly 300 bottles of Italian wine per barrel. And that was less than half of the vineyards production. Another 500 barrels were kept at another location and the winery employs dozens of huge, steel tanks.

"We produce 4.5 million bottles every year," Baldinelli said. "It's a very huge quantity."

In the slick, glass showroom afterwards, we sampled six of the vineyards finest wines. And we all walked away carrying bottles to take back to America.

Dekker, the Dutchman, purchased 12 bottles of the Sassi Neri wine from La Terrazza.

"We'll drink two or three every few months and then come back next year!" he said.

It was an admirable plan.

"Le Marche is a wonderful place," he continued. "But I think if you return in 10 years it will be a very different place, for better or worse."

- G. Miller

Healing shawls warm tourists

WE ALL WATCH the pouring rain as we stand shivering under a long portico in the town of Loreto. Berit, wearing a black halter-top, finds a little blue blanket on a rack and slings it over her tan bare shoulders.

"What are you doing?" I ask, surprised and somewhat sickened that she is snuggling into a random blanket.

"I'm covering myself so I can go in the Church," she replies indignantly. "I didn't know we were going to a church today or else I would have worn something else."

We wander ahead under the portico with no real destination.

"I don't think that's for the Church," I continue, not really ready to let Berit commit to a summer of body lice.

"Yes it is, they were all hanging there," she says pointing to a small rack.

I look around. No one else is draped in a blanket. I look at the church entrance and don't see a single person exiting with the blue cover-up. But we continue walking.

Our teacher George walks up, motions towards her covered shoulders and says, "Hey Berit. Where'd you get that?"

"Oh my gosh, I got it over there! It's to go in the church," she snaps frustrated that she has to justify her blanket to yet another inquisitive person.

Annie laughs, "Are you sure?"

Inspecting the blanket Berit notices little white designs with the initials UNITALSI.

Naturally, none of us know what this means, since it's not in our pocketsize Italian phrasebook, pathetically our only form of communication.

Around us there are dozens of elderly people, most of them sitting quietly in wheelchairs with others on plastic seats. Nurses in crisp white uniforms with little white caps wander around, kneeling down and smiling as they readjust the seniors' blankets.

I feel like I'm on the set of a movie: the nurses' costumes are too white, their smiles are too sincere, the old people look too frail and we definitely do not belong. Four American girls in flip flops and t-shirts, one wrapped in a found blanket, all of us staring and curious.

"Did they come here to get better?" I ask aloud.

The only thing we know about this town is it's a pilgrimage site. No one answers me; we're all too confused and uncomfortable to make sense of the scene before us.

Despite my protests, Berit wears the blanket into the church, the way she believes the blanket is intended to be worn. Inside we each get little pamphlets describing Loreto and the pilgrimages.

As we walk out of the church I hear Berit,

"Oh my God, Ewww," she exclaims, staring down at the brochure

Under "Shrine of the House of the Sick" subtitle she reads about UNITALSI, an organization that helps the sick pilgrims who travel from all over the world to Loreto to seek comfort and relief from their suffering.

Already Berit is holding the blanket with two outstretched fingers as far away from her body as possible with a look of disgust.

Quietly, with a scrunched face she returns the blanket to the rack she originally found it hanging from, located right next to the gathering of sick, elderly people in wheelchairs.

- Philly Petronis

Almost the biggest mistake ever

THEY CALL THEM ricciarelli cookies and they are the tastiest cookies in the world.

Really.
The ones I ate were at the Pirri Rolando Pasticceria in Loreto. The soft, maleable, feather-light cookies tasted like amaretto and sugar and they melted in my mouth.
I started with five cookies and an espresso but I had to have more.
I approached the woman at the counter and asked, "Un quatro kilo, per favore?"
She laughed for a second and then said in Italian, "Do you want 400 or 500 cookies, because that is how many four kilo's will get you. You want a 'quarto kilo,' no?"
"Oh," I replied with a smile. I had meant a quarter kilo. "Si."
Then I watched her gently toss 33 cookies into a paper bag.
I should have stuck with the four kilo's.

- G. Miller

Get the room with a view

YOU WOULD THINK THAT at the top of the highest point for miles, on a mountain that overlooks the beautiful blue waters of the Adriatic Sea, there would be some sort of lookout point for tourists.

Well, on the top of Monte Conero, there isn't.
We drove the winding roads to the top and all we found was an old church that is now attached to a luxury hotel.
Behind the hotel are woods where you can hear the sounds of splashing water from the sea several hundred feet below.

But there is only one small place where you can view the Adriatic. It is through a ten foot clearing, near a precarious railing, a few hundred yards from the parking area.

That said, the hotel looked very nice - swimming pool, tennis courts, several restaurant options. And from the hotel rooms, there seemed like there would be a fine view of all points south.

- G. Miller

Beat the system -- tan for free

ON ONE HAND, Corallo's Seaside Village is a luxurious beach resort with palm trees, a volleyball court, whirlpools, umbrellas and chairs, multiple restaurants, outdoor seating, numerous cabana's, a gelato stand, foosball tables, kayaks, several children's pools and a wide, beautiful pebble beach.

You could spend days there, soaking in the sun and entertaining yourself with the various amenities.

On the other hand, everything at Corallo's costs money, even simply sitting on a chair on the beach. An umbrella and a seat by the Adriatic Sea will run you 15 Euro for the day. Kayaks can be rented for 10 Euro per hour. Using the changing room will cost you 5 Euro.

Unlike back in the United States, most Italian beaches are operated by private businesses that charge for beach use. At Corallo's, you even have to pay for use of their ping pong table.

To skirt the rules, you can always park your towel on the sliver of land closest to the water. Most Italian beaches consider that space communal and therefore, free.

And that way, you can still get drinks at the bar and use their bathroom.

- G. Miller

Dance like no one is watching

IN THE LITTLE MERMAID, the protagonist Ariel trades her voice for a chance to have legs and go ashore. To justify this trade, the evil witch – Ursula - convinces Ariel that she doesn't need her voice because, "You have your looks, your pretty face, and don't underestimate the importance of body language."

I think of this scene when visiting a foreign country because although I have not lost my voice, it's not of much use when I can't speak the language. In order to overcome my lack of voice, I simply take Ursula's advice and use body language.

Going dancing is an automatic icebreaker.

As far as I'm concerned nothing helps overcome the language barrier better than a little Shakira.

Babaloo is said to be a hotspot not far from Camerano for young adults and Wednesday nights are free for the ladies. Another club that's right on the beach in Numana is Cavalluccio di Mare. It has a Tropical theme with grass-roofed huts sprinkled around the dance floor.

Dancing is a way to get a glimpse into the culture. You can observe the way men approach women in social situations.

Even at a less touristy nightclub the drinks can cost six or seven U.S. dollars. The locals don't seem to mind buying them for girls occasionally and maybe this has to do with how much they drink.

Europeans are more of a social drinking community. They don't usually drink to get drunk - which is often the case with American college students.

Another standard with Italian nightlife is that going to the club usually means you don't go until midnight and you don't leave for home until five in the morning.

- Caitlyn Slivinski

The Lessons

EDITOR'S NOTE: Today's headline is stolen from one of the greatest baseball players of all time, Satchel Paige. Here is his full quote: "Work like you don't need the money, love like you've never been hurt and dance like no one is watching."

Pure genius.

Even the warriors were bored

DAVE MAIALETTI WAS skeptical all along.

He hates Renaissance Festivals back home. He figured he would hate the famed Medieval Festival in Offagna, too. But I made him go. I promised there would be fireworks.

So we went to Offanga and watched jousting, archery competitions, mandolin playing and flag throwing. Honestly, it was pretty lame. Like Disneyland lame.

The crowd sat in steel bleachers, far removed from the action. We could barely see anything.

But we knew we would be able to see the fireworks from just about anywhere. And the thought of the colors illuminating the 15th century castle were enough to keep us interested (plus we paid 8 Euro to get into the city, and 2 Euro for parking).

The archery competition dragged and dragged and was followed by sword fighting and then speeches.

By midnight, more than an hour after the fireworks were scheduled, there were no fireworks.

So we left. Disappointed.

"Now I know," Dave said. "I hate Renaissance Festivals back home and Medieval Festivals in Italy."

- G. Miller

Wine and walking in a pleasant piazza

THE UMANI RONCHI WINERY distributes 4.5 million bottles of wine per year to locations around the world, with only 20% of their delicious product staying in Italy.

And if you visit the facilities, conveniently located on SS16 (one of the major roads), they'll let you drink a lot of tasty wine.

For free.

It's a great way to pass the hot summer days here in Le Marche.

In the evening, you can stroll the cobblestone streets in the lively medieval city Osimo.

You can find old men sitting along the wall of City Hall near the main piazza, younger people relaxing at Bar Diana's outdoor cafe, children playing soccer near the Diocese Museum and a whole varity of people wandering near the sculpted garden by the scenic overlook.

The scenic overlook, with its cool sea breeze wafting in, is probably about 15 degrees cooler than in the city center.

With tons of shops, restaurants, cafes, gelaterias and friendly people (the gelato seller tried to teach us Italian), Osimo is a wonderful place to visit.

- G. Miller

Riding on the escalator of life

IN GUIDEBOOKS, OSIMO IS SAID to be a city of art, history, and tradition.

Not to be skeptical but this sounds like every town in Le Marche.

To me, what stands out in Osimo is how technology is incorporated into the city's life.

Walking around we immediately find an escalator.

"Weird, an escalator – where does it go?" I question.

"Is it free?" asks Ann.

It is a reasonable question since even tap water at a restaurant has a price in Europe.

"It's definitely free," Philly says and I agree as I watch the townspeople of Osimo get on without depositing any Euro.

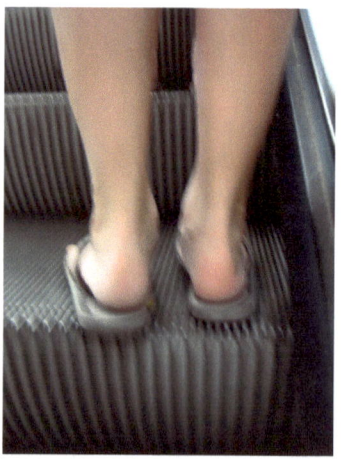

We hop on and take a short ride to the bottom of the hill, down the side of the city walls. Right in front of us is another unusual sight for these small Le Marche towns. A funicular!

"What is that?" Ann says out loud to no one in particular.

"I don't know the name," I answer, "But I've been on one before in Pittsburgh. Let's go."

Hesitantly, we approach the funicular doors, which open beckoning us to enter.

"Are you sure this is free?" Ann doubts and looks at us.

But Berit has already made up her mind that we're going to take the plunge. She coerces us to get on with her and we ride to the bottom.

"How are we going to get back up?" Philly questions.

"The same way we got down," I say but not totally trusting myself.

We thought something magical might await us at the end of our ride but instead we find a parking lot. We walk around a little and take pictures in front of a relief map of Osimo that's mounted on the wall.

Deciding to go back to the center of town, we easily figure out that the funicular will take us back up and we ascend.

In the narrow streets of Osimo, we hear American music coming from above. This is a strange experience because the apartments in this medieval city look so old but pop music explodes out its windows.

Ann listens carefully and sings along, "Shake it like a Polaroid picture."

And we do.

After a fun afternoon in this town we get ready to meet back in the piazza. Berit and Philly get ahead of Ann and I and they quickly disappear. We later find out that they had stepped into a candy store and found quite a treat.

It turns out that Osmio is one of the few places that we have found a delicious chewy fruit candy called Dietorelle.

There are many other attractions in Osimo like the City Hall, the Diocese Museum, the Cathedral of Saint Leopard and the Dance and Ballet festival.

But if I had to tell you the top three things to do in Osimo, it would be to check out the high-tech vertical public transportation, take pictures of the view and indulge in some sweet, chewy Dietorelle.

- Caitlyn Slivinski

Dinner straight from the Sea

I REALLY DO LOVE working for my food.

For some reason a bag of naked green pistachios don't taste as good as they do after being pried through their a hard shell.

The tongue testing mouth maneuvers needed to de-shell a sunflower seed makes an equally admirable and rewarding snack.

However, as I stare down at the seven "grilled shrimp" that look more like dwarfed lobsters on my dinner plate, I am caught off guard.

I had ordered a fish dish figuring that it would be fresh and delicious, served in the town of Sirolo. After all, I could see the home of my future dinner, the Adriatic Sea, from the town's main piazza.

I am starving and now I have to make my way through each hard red shell and scrape out the meager meat inside. How does one go about eating these without totally grossing out their surrounding fellow diners?

I glance to my left at Berit, who has previously voiced her repulsion towards all seafood. She stares down in polite silence that does little to mask her disgust.

To my right Annie looks at me apprehensively. Highly allergic to shellfish and without her medication in Italy, my plate is essentially a death wish.

I tentatively take a shrimp and begin sawing, cracking and crunching through its little body. Pink meat is exposed in the tail. I question the edibility of the squishy brown guts in the abdomen.

An eyeball and antennae break off.

I'm reminded of a high school biology class. I crack another shrimp and a piece lands on Annie's shirt. Some ends up in my hair. It's going to be a long dinner.

By the end my plate looks like a war zone. Legs, eyeballs, antennae, cracked bodies and guts are smeared across my plate.

For all that work I'm still not full and thinking ahead to a gelato dessert.

All that takes is a spoon.

- Philly Petronis

EDITOR'S NOTE: The seven shrimp were huge (about 8 inches long), unadorned and whole. They appeared to be taken directly from the Sea, grilled and placed on Philly's plate.

And she ate them all.

Her determination was impressive.

Beauty in the breakdown

FROM MY TRIP TO ITALY, I've learned two things about traveling: there's no place like home when you finally want to get there, and sometimes it's okay to loosen the purse strings (and your vocal cords).

Berit and I began talking about leaving a day before it was scheduled to happen.

"It's so close...if we were staying for another week, that would be one thing, but we're leaving tomorrow. I'm ready to go." Berit explained to me over lunch the afternoon before our planned departure.

I wholeheartedly agreed with her rationale. By the end of the trip, I felt like I was killing time. I could no longer plan a weekend in Croatia or Rome or even spend the night at a nearby beach. There were things — deadlines, farewell parties, goodbyes — holding us in one place.

Like Berit, I was ready to go.

Berit and I awoke at 4:30 on a muggy Saturday morning to leave for the airport. Our flight left Ancona at 6:45 and landed in Milan at 8. We were scheduled to leave Milan and fly to Amsterdam, then leave Amsterdam for John F. Kennedy airport, bringing us home by 3:30 New York time. Berit and I had booked the same three-stop flight by chance and for the same reason: to save an extra 200 dollars rather than booking a direct flight.

We left Ancona on time and both slept the entire way. We arrived in Milan as scheduled, easily found our gate for the next flight, and even managed to buy some chocolate treats for loved ones.

So far, our trip was off to a good (and stress-free) start.

What happened next can only be described as a nightmare.

We boarded the Alltalia plane and weren't exactly surprised to find out that we weren't sitting next to each other, just disappointed. I threw myself into a Hello! Magazine, studying Mickey Rooney's girlfriend's drunken antics like there was going to be a test later and waited for take-off.

After more than forty-five minutes of the plane being completely immobile, it finally started to move. The plane circled the runway twice before the captain came over the loudspeaker and announced something in Italian. I watched the other passenger's reactions to try and figure out what he said. There was eye-rolling and teeth grinding, but nothing too outrageous, and I figured since no one was exiting the plane, the scenario couldn't be too bad.

Then, from a few rows back, I heard a high pitch scream. Several other passengers and I averted our attention toward the back of the plane, where a woman was trudging down the aisle ahead of two stewardesses who were trying to calm her down. "Tranquity," they whispered quietly as the woman stormed on. I glanced around nervously. No one seemed to have any clue what was going on. I felt butterflies begin to flutter in my stomach.

The plane started moving again, this time, I noticed, without the hysterical woman in her seat. I took several deep breaths, trying to ignore the couple next to me who were chanting some spiritual chant in an attempt, I'm guessing, to calm their own nerves.

The plane moved at top speed for less than ten seconds before stopping. The pilot came over the loudspeaker once again, and this time his announcement made all the passengers began grabbing their luggage and exiting the plane.

After finding Berit, together we realized that there was almost no possible way we were to going to land in Amsterdam in time to make our connecting flight. Panic sunk in.

We waited on several different hour-long lines before getting any real answers. Every time we thought we were getting somewhere, we were instructed to change lines again. Over the next seven hours, Berit and I met an Italian couple traveling to the United States for their honeymoon, a Canadian couple who was told that Alltalia only flew to Calgary (their destination) once a week, and a Puerto Rican woman with three kids who had been stuck in the airport for three days. It was comforting to know that we weren't the only ones going through this breakdown.

Within minutes of being in the presence of the Puerto Rican woman, Berit and I knew exactly why she was still there: she was too polite and passive.

Pushing our way to the front of the fourth line we were directed to, Berit and I calmly explained our situation. "You cancelled the flight, we want to go home, make it happen" was how we summed it up by this point. We had told our sad tale so many times and were beginning to worry that no one was actually listening. Just sending us to another line.

But when the incredibly rude and apathetic woman from Alltalia informed us that all flights to the United States were overbooked and we probably wouldn't get a flight home until August 6th, Berit and I realized that we controlled our own fate. Nodding patiently and saying little was going to keep us in the

Milan airport for days, even a week. Screaming and making this Alltalia employee realize that her life would actually benefit once we were in the air, crossing the Atlantic Ocean was what was going to get us home.

Ten minutes later, we had the tickets for tomorrow's flight to Newark in our hands, as well as two free vouchers for a nearby hotel.

I'm not one to condone such aggressive behavior, but when you're stuck in a foreign country, being treating like you are a moron, it's okay and sometimes necessary to go a little nuts.

And Berit and I agree, from now on, we will ALWAYS book a direct flight.

- Ann Curran

No coffee for you!

THE TRAIN SYSTEM IN ITALY can be terribly confusing and also an extremely interesting means of people watching.

Before embarking on a weekend trip to Rome my friends and I decide that the best way for us to reach the Eternal City would be to take the train. An easy three hour ride from Ancona to Rome, it seemed the most obvious choice.

The first train available happens to be the local, meaning that it will take a bit longer and make several more stops than the more expensive and spacious Eurostar. Eager to begin our trip we decide to take it, happy that it is only costing us €13.

Walking onto the train the hot stuffy July air fills the cars.

"Please tell me there is air conditioning", says Annie.

Well, none of the cars seems to be air conditioned so we sit down in the closest available seats.

Once the train begins to move, the conductor makes his way to our car. In a blur of Italian he indicates that we have forgotten to stamp our tickets before boarding the train.

Oh yeah.

According to our conductor this offense is punishable with a € 20 fine. However, he will not charge us and instead writes a rather lengthy blur of Italian words at the top of our ticket (I am assuming this excuses us from forgetting to stamp our tickets before boarding the train).

He then goes into another long incomprehensible rant. My friends and I stare blankly, wishing we understood him and nodding our heads. What could he be saying? By this time the air has thickened to an almost unbearable cloud of heat. My entire body, as with the rest of the individuals sitting in our car, is covered in a thin layer of sweat. It is awful.

Annie decides to look and see if there is a snack car to buy a bottle of water, only to return with a look of shock and embarrassment.

"There's air conditioning in the other cars," she says.

Ahhhh. Maybe that's what the conductor was trying to tell us.

We quickly move to the next car, invading the space of a young Italian girl who does not look pleased to be sharing the seats around her with a bunch of sweaty Americans.

The crisp cold air envelopes our bodies and instantly I cool down. I decide to go with Annie on another search for water and we head toward the end of the car.

While on our hunt we see a broad range of unusual-looking characters. We can't help but burst into a fit of giggles as we try to steady ourselves while walking down the aisles of the swaying train.

The first is a young boy, perhaps the equivalent of the American adolescent Goth. He sits in his seat with a sword pointed upwards in between his legs. He slowly strokes the blade while looking around at the other members of his car. Although I laugh, I walk past him as quickly as possible - he is more scary than funny.

Next we pass a woman who seems to have lost her modesty after becoming a mother. She sits with her her shirt around her neck and her young infants mouth attached to her breast. Her eyes are closed and she appears to be asleep.

Lastly, we pass a car that appears to be a scene from a movie. Several young men, all dressed casually, sit facing each other on the left side of the train car. They are singing in Italian and looking as though they are having a party.

At last we make our way to the end of the train where Annie proceeds with one of the sole Italian words we have learned to master.

"Café?" she asks, looking for the café car.

The conductor looks confused. Perhaps we are not as talented as we think. Annie stares at me blankly as we often do when we are at a loss for words because not knowing any Italian has, in fact, often left as at a complete loss for words.

Resorting to the universal sign for eating, I start acting like I am putting food into my mouth. The conductor laughs and shakes his head no.

There is no food cart on this train.

- Berit Baugher

EDITOR'S NOTE: The top image comes courtesy of Jennifer Adams, a Berry College student who was a member of the 2006 Camerano Project.

Why travel?

WE STARTED THE DAY by climbing the tower of the well-preserved medieval castle in Offagna and then drove to Jesi for lunch.

Of course, Jesi was essentially closed because of pausa (Italian siesta), so as soon as we finished our midday meals we dashed off to a vineyard in nearby Morro D'Alba.
The vineyard was a real treat — air condition and free wine. Nothing could have been better on a blazing summer day. We stayed for nearly three hours and then drove to Senigallia to meet a friend for drinks.
Well, drinks turned into dinner, which lead to a long stroll on the beach, and by the time we returned to our base camp (after driving in circles for a while when we got lost), a 15-hour day had elapsed.
Then we ventured out on a similar journey the next day.
It was exhausting.
A few days after those marathon adventures, Philly posed an interesting question to the group, "Why do you like to travel?"
It was a valid query and one that seems to carry even more weight now — in this age of global terrorism, in an era when getting anywhere by plane is anything but simple and convenient and getting anywhere by car will cost you a month's mortgage payment.
Why would you want to leave your comfortable home to wait in line for hours at airport security, then sleep in a hotel of questionable repute, eat all of your meals at unknown restaurants and waste a tank of gas driving around some city you're visiting because it looked good in some glossy magazine?
It's not like it's cheap or anything. And in many parts of the world, like here in Italy, most people don't even speak English.
Yet we all vacation and travel to some extent, whether it's down the shore, across the country or around the world. We travel to get away from the daily grind, to forget about our everyday existences, to leave the cell phones behind and ignore the e-mail.
I find traveling to be even more rewarding, beyond simple escapism.
My answer to the Philly's question was, "I like to travel because I want to know everything about everything."
I want to know why Italian stores close all afternoon. I want to know why there are rocks on roofs of homes there. I want to know why there are so many castles in such close proximity of each other. I want to know why the wine in Le Marche has a

higher alcohol content than most other places.

I want to know how life is different somewhere else and why.

From the top of the tower in Offagna, we could see Osimo, Loreto and Castelfidardo, three other fortress-like cities perched on different hills in different directions, separated only by a few kilometers. The castle towns, we learn, were established during the Middle Ages as a ring of protection for the primary city of the region, Ancona, which has the Adriatic Sea on its other flank.

The salty air wafting in off the Adriatic Sea cools the grapes that grow in Le Marche but it is the blistering Italian sun that gives them their intensity. The copious quantity of sunshine helps ripen the grapes and increases their sugar content. The high sugar levels make for higher alcohol percentages in the region's wines.

The hot sun is also the reason why Italians close shop in the afternoons. Most people arrive early for work, then close at 12:30 for afternoon "pausa," and then re-open around 4. In towns closer to the sea or further down the peninsula, the shops may not re-open until 5 or 5:30. Then people stay at work until 7 or 8.

It is just too hot to do anything during the midday hours. Outside of the larger cities, much of Italy is a ghost town on hot summer afternoons.

The winds can really pick up in Italy, with currents blowing in from both the Mediterranean and the Adriatic seas. A good gust will blow the orange, baked-brick tiles right off a person's home.

Unless you set some heavy rocks on top of them, that is.

During dinner in Senigallia, Philly sighed and then lamented, "I miss big coffee."

In Italy, even the largest serving of coffee is less than one-third the size of the average Starbucks variety.

"It's terrible, the American coffee," our friend, Carlo Cleri, replied.

Cleri, who is an organizer of the local Slow Foods chapter in Italy, then proclaimed, "I hate Coke, too."

And the girls gasped as though he had just burned an American flag.

"Slow food means the opposite of fast food," Cleri explained. "In food, you can find history, culture."

There are thousands of food products in Italy – from meats and cheeses to wines – that are only produced in small pockets of the country ... and nowhere else in the world.

"We think diversity makes everything better," Cleri said.

It is also the best reason to travel.

- G. Miller

The Locals
Interactions with Marchesi

- Crystals, Valium and sound advice for female travelersEvery night is ladies' night
- The man with the machete means no harm
- Keep moving, there's nothing to see here
- Fantastico nights with Italian boys
- A room and a scare - and a reason to celebrate
- Sgarbato girl makes a friend
- My date with Moses
- Hello God, it's me Caitlyn
- Patience (and a nice hat) pays off
- Mio vino e vostro vino
- It was a pleasure!

Valium and shocking advice

"NERVOUS FLYER," I THINK to myself as I strain my eyes to inconspicuously watch the woman on my left.

She takes a small object out of a little woven drawstring bag and begins methodically rubbing it, with closed eyes while she rocks in her cramped airplane seat. It's not until she dangles it from a short fishing line and swings it hypnotically back and forth that I realize the object is a rectangular clear crystal.

After a minute or two the woman turns to me, "It tells me we will not take off."

Although my initial reaction to the future telling powers of a rock would normally be skeptical, I had already endured four hours and two failed trips to the runway on a plane full of hungry, tired passengers. I am in desperate need of some sort of explanation or definitive resolution, regardless of the source.

I let out an exasperated sigh, audibly accepting the possible truth of her statement. Half out of boredom and half out of curiosity I point to her clenched fist and ask, "How does it work?"

It is as if I asked her how babies are made. An expression of discomfort and surprise takes over her face. Taking a deep breath, she sits back in her seat.

I am ready to give up all hope of finding an answer when she turns back to me and slowly replies in her thick Swiss accent, "I ask it question and it tell me yes or no."

Ten minutes later we are taxiing for a third time to the runway. The pilot has reassured the passengers that after refueling a second time, the crew has fixed the problem.

As the relieved passengers chat in excitement, the woman turns to me once again and asks, "Are you nervous?"

Obviously at this point my nerves are enough to potentially fill a vomit bag but right away I reply, "No."

"I am. I have bad feeling. This flight," she says, pointing at the plane's cockpit while nodding her head in assurance. She closes her eyes and crosses her fleshy arms across her dragonfly patterned linen dress. "There is something wrong with plane still. I have feeling."

"Could I ignore these potential final words," I wonder as the plane engines emit their deafening roar. "Was this sense of doom and feeling of helpless dread common to all plane crash victims?"

What to do? Vomit? Freak out and get off the flight? Join forces with the crystal lady and demand they check the plane again?

With no other option, I opt for Valium and cover my head with the navy-colored plane blanket. A slow death due to suffocation from a stale smelling felt square won't be so bad.

I am awakened by the sound of applause from the passengers, an unnecessary and extravagant gesture that never fails to cause personal humiliation. I rush off the plane to catch my connecting flight.

As I say a hurried farewell to my seatmate she leaves me with one lasting piece of advice, "Good luck with life. Whatever you do don't get pregnant too young."

With a nervous laugh, I assure her this was not the plan and wave goodbye, hoping it was the crystal that advised her to give such a warning.

- Philly Petronis

Every night is ladies' night?

IT'S NINE O'CLOCK IN THE EVENING, you've already had dinner, and you're in Italy — quick, what do you do? Well if you've been to Europe before you know that the only thing to do is unwind with an authentic glass of wine... or two or three.

With the summer evening air setting the perfect atmosphere we find a quaint Trattoria called Strologo and take a seat outside. One problem. There are only three chairs and four of us.

Behind a beaded curtain we see a waiter and we catch his attention. "Scusa, un autre (we pointed to the other chairs)" we explain that we'll be needing an additional chair. After this mini game of charades he understands and disappears behind the beaded curtain.

Waiting on the small patio outside, we observe the diners inside. They are loudly enjoying the huge plates in front of them. That visual, plus the aroma of fresh pasta sauce floating through that curtain is enough to make my stomach growl...even though I had already eaten dinner.

Our waiter returns with the chair and we promptly order a bottle of wine, but it sounds more French than Italian, "une bouteille vino bianchi, per favore?"

We can see the amusement in his eyes and he corrects us. He asks if we would like a bottle of water with that. This is the first Italian question we understand and so with enthusiasm we all shout "NON GRAZIE!"

No sooner does our waiter burst into laughter than we realize that our enthusiasm has been misunderstood as enthusiasm against water, as if we are saying forget the water bring us our wine! But it's too late to explain because he has already disappeared back behind the beads becoming only a silhouette in the noisy restaurant.

After a few glasses the time seems to just evaporate and so does the wine because before we know it, our waiter is back asking if we'd like another bottle. We shrug and agree - I mean we are in Italy after all and we wouldn't want to offend our new friend.

During our second bottle of wine is when we just can't take it anymore. We have to surrender to the smell of food still taunting us from inside although the customers have long since gone home. We call our waiter once again and ask him for a menu. And once again he laughs in our face. It's a friendly laugh though, so we don't mind.

But we can't quite figure out what we're doing wrong this time. He explains but it's to no avail since we clearly aren't masters in the Italian language.

Charades ensue and we finally get it. The kitchen is closed and our waiter thinks it's oh so funny that we were even asking since it's eleven at night. I guess the Italians are immune to the late night munchies.

The light behind the beaded curtain goes out and we decide we might have over-stayed our welcome. We finish our drinks and ask for the bill.

When our waiter appears through that curtain for this last time that night, he smiles and shoos us away. We look at each other with confusion and then restate our request for the check.

"Il conto?" we say again, figuring that once again we were butchering the Italian language.

He shakes his head and shoos us away again.

No bill? Free wine all night? We thank him and bid our goodbyes. Walking away we announce to the waiter, "Lunedi we'll be back!"

- Caitlyn Slivinski

EDITOR'S NOTE: We know the Italian words are spelled wrong and used improperly in this story ... that's part of what makes it funny.

Machete man means no harm

SLOWLY WE MAKE OUR WAY down the side of the hill, following the park trail.

Completely unaware of what lay before us, Caitlyn, Philly and I decide to continue on the path even though it means passing - or should I say trespassing - through a small hole cut in a seemingly endless barbed wire fence. We each hesitantly take a step through the hole, only to be caught within the next minute.

The air is rich with the smell of soil and the sun beats down on my black shirt.

An older man, who looks to be in his 70's, appears on our left. With the face of a farmer aged by many years of hard labor under the Italian sun, he spits out a seemingly agitated jumble of Italian words.

Because our Italian language capabilities don't stretch much further than, "Ciao," and "Grazie," we turn to each other in utter confusion.

Who is this man? Is this his land? And most importantly look at the size of that machete in his right hand.

In an act of defense we silently agree to resort to playing the role of ignorant lost traveler.

"Piazza?" one of us squeaks out.

It's the only local landmark we know.

The man's sternness evaporates and after several words of Italian, he ends his sentence with, "Americano?"

He signals for us to follow him on the path toward what appears to be his home. The man walks over to a small wooden hut and pulls open a door revealing a room full of chickens.

"Pollo" he says waiting for us to repeat.

And we return with, "Pollo?"

He then walks us into a large run down building and flicks a switch that triggers a dim shaky light hung from the ceiling. He motions for us to walk towards the numerous cages—pulling one open and sticking his hand in, only to reappear with a small naked bunny no bigger than the size of my palm. He motions for me to put my hand out and the small creature wiggles in my grasp.

"Due giorni" he says, explaining that the bunny is two days old.

"Ahhh," we respond, repeating his phrase, followed by the American equivalent.

We pass the newborn around and glance in the numerous cages of rabbits lining the perimeter of the room. On our way toward the driveway the man points toward a green car peaking out of a partially closed garage.

"Ford," he says pointing toward the car. "American. Good."

Yes we agree, nodding in unison.

At last something we can relate to. We continued toward the driveway only to hear the snarls of a large cream colored dog. He stands between us and the road, with his teeth bared and saliva dripping down the side of his face.

The man walks toward the dog and grabs a hold of his collar while waving goodbye.

- Berit Baugher

Nothing to see here

WITHOUT KNOWING THE ITALIAN word for fitting room I hold the shirts I picked out up to my torso. I point to the shirt, point to myself and, in English, say to the saleswoman, "Try on?'

It's Wednesday, market day in Camerano. There are dozens of stands - open from 9am until 12:30 in the afternoon - with racks of discounted clothing lining the piazza. It is a scene replicated in small towns across Italy on a daily basis.

The woman answers something back in Italian and them motions for me to follow her.

We take a few steps over to a large white van, which she uses to transport her clothing products from town to town, from market day to market day.

As she opens the van, all I can think is, "What is going on?"

She points her thin, tan finger to the open door and looks at me. Shrugging my shoulders I climb into this huge unmarked van.

"Is she kidnapping me?" I wonder.

Once inside I see that a white tarp has been hung in the interior of the van and a mirror is leaning against the driver's seat. I finally realize it's a make-shift fitting room and I try on my shirts.

Sure the tarp doesn't cover all the windows and the people of Camerano perusing the market this morning can probably see me changing but you learn that the Wednesday market is a, "When in Rome ..." type of thing.

After trying on my shirts I exit the van and practically bump into the vender. She asks, "Va bene?"

No, sadly, they are not good.

I shake my head and hand her the shirts, slightly defeated.

- Caitlyn Slivinski

Fantastico nights with Italians

WE WALK INTO THE BAR that our roommate Kiley has dubbed the Havana Club - because of the vintage sign on the back wall that reads just that - and we have our first encounter with the locals.

They're getting rippin' drunk and we're looking for trouble.

A guy that looks about my age — 20 - and seems like he's a few drinks deep passes by. He's sporting an Italia jersey and I scan my mind for something to say.

"Mi piace," I blurt it out and point to his shirt since, "I like," is the first thing to pop into my head.

Instead of being impressed by my language skills, he looks back at me and with a devilish smile asks in Italian, "You like my shirt or you like me?"

I roll my eyes to disguise my embarrassment then quickly tug on his shirt to clear up the misunderstanding and scurry away.

Meanwhile back at the table, my friends pore over the menu, picking out fancy drinks to try. About to take a look myself, I hear my new "mi piace" friend yelling.

I spin around as he shoves a glass of red wine in my hand; it matches the one in his own.

In harmony, we shout, "Salute!"

Then he introduces himself as Roberto. It takes about half a second for his friends to catch on, approach Roberto, and ask him "who's your buddy?"

Well, they said something in Italian. I assume that's what it was.

Another hand is thrust into mine. His name is Mauro and he speaks English. Kind of. He explains that there is a beach nearby called Black Rock and that after the bar he and his friends go and spend the night in their sleeping bags.

Sleeping bag is a word Mauro does not know in Italian. He holds his hands up in prayer position and tilts his head against them. Roberto yawns like he's tired. Mauro then puts his hands out like he's holding something at knee-height and jumps into it. Roberto puts his hands the same way but after jumping he pinches his fingers together and makes an upward motion and a "zzzip" sound.

"Ohh, a sleeping bag?" I finally guess.

Roberto nods and repeats, "Fantastico!"

It seems that everything Roberto says is followed by, "Fantastico!"

The beach is fantastico, the wine, the sleeping bag. It's his favorite word, and mine too because I understand it.

After some convincing, my American friends and I agree to take advantage of our time here because we knew we don't have a moment to waste this month. These days go and they go fast.

Before I know it we're all navigating our way on foot down a path in the pitch-black forest that leads down to place the Italians kept calling, "Fantastico!"

It takes a brutal twenty minutes - stumbling in the dark - to reach the bottom but once we get down there it's worth it. Think Cape Cod with people sitting around campfires and the waves crashing on the shore — only better.

Better because we're in Italy.

There's Italian chatter, the waves are waves of the Adriatic and it is the perfect place to watch the sunrise... I learned this at 6:27 am when I'm woken up to watch it.

My contacts are glued to my eyeballs because I've slept with them in - like I know I'm not supposed to do. Squinting, I crawl out of the two sleeping bags my Italian friends had lent to me to make sure I slept comfortably. The soft sand cradles my feet and I join my friends at the shoreline to watch the day break.

Everything looks different now: the campfires are just blackened logs, the beach is barren and the waves are the only sound on the Black Rock Beach this morning.

Slowly we walk back towards to the path that led us down the night before. We struggle up through the forest and I think, "I'm glad I didn't think about this last night "

Had I known it was this steep and arduous, I may never have walked down. I would've missed out on a fantastico night.

- Caitlyn Slivinski

A room and a scare

IT REALLY LOOKS LIKE a scene from The Shining, a movie that haunts me.

I've had the same scary dream at least three or four times a year since I was 8-years old. And now, while I'm trying to relax and clear my head in Italy, I find myself face-to-face with my nightmare.

Only this time, it's reality.

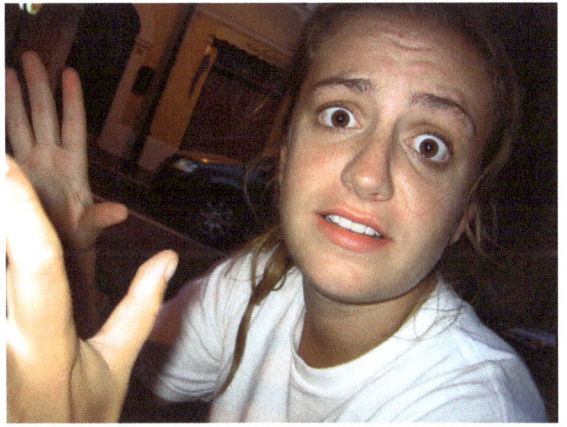

After an hour in the car and what seems like ages of aimlessly walking up and down different streets, the girls and I finally locate this cozy hotel we had stayed in the previous summer. There, at the front desk sits the creepiest man I have ever seen in real life, smiling, like he's been waiting for our arrival.

I suggest unless you enjoy a good scare (or you're vacationing with a 6'6 250 pound linebacker to protect you), make sure you feel comfortable with the receptionist at the Hotel Orfeo BEFORE you give him your passport.

His skin is sunken in and swollen at the same time, loose by his fleshy cheeks and tight around his olive shaped eyes. One eye is lazy and both are bloodshot. His pupils are dilated. Countless veins cover his forearms as though there are clothespins actually pinching his skin and forcing it to be so taut. His sinister grin exposes crooked stained teeth.

"Americane?" he asks with slurred speech.

I shudder.

I watch as my friends struggle to communicate with the man, shocked that they are willingly handing over their passports to a man whose appearance alone has given me goosebumps.

And I'm beginning to realize that had he asked for their driver's licenses, credit card and social security numbers, and original birth certificates, they would have obliged. Nothing scares these girls.

After we check in, we climb the two flights of stairs to our room. Everything looks different from last year. The once rose-colored walls have darkened to the shade of blood. The stench of the hotel is stale and putrid. It smells of death.

Once we are out of earshot, I let my friends have it, "Um, was anyone else like totally freaked out by that guy?"

The girls giggle and agree that his looks were not only unfortunate but downright frightening. They also comment on how funny it is that we seem to be the only guests staying in the hotel.

Hilarious.

While I have absolutely no problem being the wet blanket of the group and demanding we leave, I was too busy studying the creep and our surroundings to notice my friends toss fifty Euro in his direction. And I get the feeling this guy's idea of a refund involves a switchblade and some rope.

When I wake up the next morning, alive and in one piece, I do a dance of celebration.

- Ann Curran

Sgarbato girl makes a friend

WHEN MY GOOD FRIEND returned home from Cabo San Luca after a week of sun, booze, and no sleep (i.e. spring break), she made sure to bring with her the perfect souvenir: a hot pink bracelet with the word "rude" stitched into a purple background.

Now to some, this may seem hostile, mean and even rude itself, but to friends who have jokingly and lovingly nicknamed the other "rude," it is in fact the perfect souvenir. When I left for Italy a few months later, I vowed to return home with a gift equally poignant.

Trudging through the damp streets of Loreto, I can't help but think the town is no different than any other city for a tourist. There are small stores that sell postcards and gelato and Italian flags, shopkeepers sweeping the outside of their shops, and a steel-colored cobblestone road connecting everything.

Yawning, I trek on, desperate to find something other than another café Americano (con latte) to revitalize my sleepy mood. That's when I spot Antonella and a little shop called Ricami Veronica.

A curious looking group had formed around what looked like five or six of the stores I had just walked by. Intrigued, I push my way through the stragglers and manage a front row seat.

A plump, warm looking woman sits on display with a blue sewing machine perched in front of her. Using her delicate fingers, she is maneuvering an off-white apron back and forth as the needle drills thick, navy thread through the cloth. It looks like an intricate, magical design from where I stand. When the woman slowly turns it right-side up for everyone to see, there is a communal gasp as the name "Nicole" suddenly appears.

I watch the next few creations in a state of awe and excitement. There is a plethora of aprons, bibs, purses, bracelets, towels, belts, and other accessories throughout the store, waiting to be personalized by the creative hand of the woman, the talented Antonella.

I quickly decide that this would be the perfect gift for my friend. Not only can I reciprocate my friend's gift with a bracelet that reads "sgarbato" (Italian for "rude"), I can also return home with a memento of the most beautiful and elaborate calligraphy I have ever seen.

Waiting to be acknowledged by Antonella proves to be more difficult than I anticipate. I figure that there is a large and cranky demand for a piece of this artwork, but I continue to be ignored and skipped over due to my lack of being able to speak Italian. I must be pushy and persistent, but I barely know how to say, "Excuse me." The other customers in the store can only be described as sgarbato.

After almost an hour, I am ready to accept defeat and leave without a bracelet. Just as I give up, Antonella saunters over and gently asks in slightly broken English how she can help. I hand her the light pink bracelet I have already picked out and a piece of scrap paper with the words "sgarbato" and "scherzo" (explaining that it was a "joke") scratched in black ink.

Antonella smiles and nods as she reads the words and returns to her seat. I watch once again as like magic she pushes and pulls the thin bracelet through the machine, and "sgarbato" eventually shines through.

She then asks for my name. I sheepishly tell her my "rude" friend's name, and she takes a green note-card, places it under her sewing machine and it reads "Andi" before I know it.

I don't know if she does this because she feels badly that I have waited for so long but I leave with the bracelet, Andi's name-card and satisfied, happy memories of an otherwise dreary day in Loreto.

- Ann Curran

My date with Moses

AT FIRST I DON'T really know how to address the three men standing before me.

My intimidation is partially due to their long baby blue tunics belted with thick white robes, and also due in part to their enthusiastic interest in anything I say.

My month long trip to Italy and undergraduate degree seem pathetic after learning they have studied in Italy for seven years, becoming fluent in five different languages, and they will be returning to their native country Zambia in seven months. There they will finish their studies and become priests.

"How old are you?" I ask one of the men hoping that maybe I still have a few years to catch up and learn at least one more language.

"Twenty-three," Moses says grinning.

I am 21. And when I tell him that, he high-fives me.

He tells me what town they are studying in. Not recognizing the name I ask him to write it on a piece of paper. After writing his address he takes the opportunity to write down his email and two phone numbers.

Then passes the paper to each of his friends who do the same.

Before handing the notebook back to me, he adds a second email address in case the first one he gave doesn't work.

While it is not a rare occurrence for me to exchange phone numbers with guys that I meet out at bars, it was only in Loreto that I had the unique experience of acquiring the digits and email addresses of not one, but three student priests.

Moses and I chat a little longer and I snap a photo of us all which I promise to email to them.

Up to then, I had found Loreto kind of boring. The Catholic church looked a lot like the others I had seen throughout Italy, the souvenir shops were pretty standard with lots of rosary beads and crosses, and the people watching was pretty weak due to the rain.

Looking for inspiration I thought the three young men could explain the town's appeal.

"Why are you visiting Loreto?" I ask Moses.

As he looks around, he laughs and doesn't answer me. Only when he looks back at me and sees my questioning expression does he realize that I'm serious.

He replies, "To see the church, to see the black Madonna, to watch the Eucharist."

His tone implied a lighthearted, "Duh."

I look over to a gathering of people at the side of the square. A bible-carrying priest leads a procession through the crowd.

"Shall we go?" he asks, motioning towards the crowd.

I stand with my new friends listening to the service, watching the people recite Italian words in unison.

"Are you Catholic?" he asks.

"No, Episcopalian."

"Oh," he says, clearly disappointed.

In an attempt to win back his respect I add, "I went to Catholic college."

"Ah ... very good," he says smiling and turning back to the service.

Curious about the black Madonna and the religious ties to Loreto I look it up in a local guide magazine when I get home.

"Talking about Loreto, it is thinking about faith," I read.

Confused about the meaning, I assume something may have been lost in the magazine's Italian to English translation. Still, I'm reminded of the student priests.

I e-mail each of them the picture and propose the plan of visiting their town. I am not envious of their lifestyle, but impressed by their dedication and it may be one of the few times I will get a guy's number and make an effort to see him again.

- Philly Petronis

Hello God, it's me, Caitlyn

LORETO IS AN HISTORIC, religious town and a host to many pilgrimages.

When we arrive, however, it's raining and doesn't seem so special.

Ducking under a doorway to stay dry we watch a monk stroll in an oversized, hooded, chocolate robe. He's dark-skinned with white hair and the robe sits heavy on his frail body.

As he passes, the most enormous thunder goes off and echoes through the city. The light above us in the entrance to the crypt flickers and Philly, Berit, and I grab onto each other and huddle against a decorative iron door behind us.

Our professor, George, looks back at us and scoffs, "Funny, because the first thing I think when I hear thunder is to get away from the metal."

We all laugh, but George admits that the thunder scared him too.

It seems everyone jumped at the sound...except the monk who is still walking towards the Bascilica, in the rain. He's sort of smiling to himself, as if he was the one who set off the ground-shaking sound.

"Was that God?" I wonder aloud, half joking.

Now in a religious state of mind, I wander onward and see a flock of ladies dressed head to toe in white. Their shoes are orthopedic-style and chunky, stockings covered their legs and a one piece jumper is their uniform. The whole outfit is bleached pure white. Each one seems busily tending to an elderly person, of which there are many.

Looking around I think, "These nuns all look so young."

I see one talking on her cell phone and wearing a lot of make-up.

Later in the day I spot a few of these nuns in a store getting custom-embroidered aprons and giggling like schoolgirls. They are throwing down money left and right.

"Things sure seem opposite here in Loreto," I say, puzzled.

It is then that a shiny object catches my eye. A small red cross on their habit lets me know that these nuns were not nuns at all.

They are nurses.

"Well that explains a lot," I comment aloud to assure myself that I wasn't going crazy.

As soon as they leave the store I watch as three nurses reach into their purses and light up cigarettes.

"Loreto nurses all smoke cigarettes?" I say to no one. "I feel like I'm in the twilight zone."

- Caitlyn Slivinski

Patience pays off

AFTER WALKING AROUND the university buildings, through crowds of people and down endless streets full of stands selling clothing, jewelry, shoes, bags, pictures and souvenirs, I am hungry.

I see a large fruit stand at the end of a street and decide to get an apple.

Never have I witnessed such a chaotic event.

I watch people shouting orders at the fruit stand employees who hurriedly walk to and from the different wooden crates of fruit. With their black fingernails caked with dirt, they grab at various fruits and plop them into bags. The bags are thrown onto a scale and coins are slammed into a small metal box.

Customers yell for firmer apples, point out bruised peaches, test grapes for seeds, ask for more and bargain to pay less.

I figure that I will get noticed by standing in front of the stand, staring down the various fruit stand employees.

No one looks at me.

Berit and Annie go off to play with a homeless man's puppies. George wanders off to shoot pictures. Caitlyn joins me on my quest to get recognized. Only after the other customers have left does the woman look at me with one of the most pissed off expressions I have ever seen.

I do my usual pointing, combined with a half mumbled attempt at saying apple, "mele," and then, "uno, uhhh."

I step forward, shift back, smile.

I use this tactic often and it usually translates roughly as, "I am a dumb American and I want one apple, please."

Of course she doesn't understand. Apparently no one comes to the stand to buy just one single piece of fruit.

People usually stock up on market day, leaving with pounds and pounds of fruit to last the following weeks, I guess. Finally after I do my routine a couple more times and Caitlyn points to a nectarine, the fruit stand woman gives us each our fruit, free of charge.

She sighs and basically shoos us away, annoyed that she even took a minute to look at us.

I walk away trying to figure out why she gave us the freebees. I figure she felt bad for our half hour wait, she wanted us to leave as quickly as possible or she pitied the hats we had bought in town and wore so proudly (despite their obvious lack of style).

- Philly Petronis

A reason to drink mid-day

I'M REMINDED OF a really clean big garage when I enter the main room of the Mancinelli Winery. Rather than cars, large stainless steel barrels that measure about 15-feet line one side of the room.

"It smells like a hangover," Annie whispers.

A short old man, owner Fabio Mancinelli, greets us warily, not knowing what to make of the four smiling girls with their male chaperone silently standing before him.

George attempts to break the ice with his paltry Italian vocabulary. Somehow he succeeds in getting across the point that we're "journalism" students.

The man's offer to allow us to taste the wines on a table next to him seems reluctant, yet once he starts pouring he's very generous passing out three different glasses refilled twice more with different red wines.

I smile after each taste, hoping that between the five of us we will be able to finish the servings.

We pass the glasses around each trying to pawn off the remaining wine by arguing about our varying tolerance levels and how much we've already had. It's an awkward position, not wanting to be drunk in the middle the day and not wanting to be rude.

Smiles are the only way I can show my reaction to the various wines' tastes. After tasting the final full-bodied red wine I'm unable to remember if its "molto buono" or "molto bene," so I resort to a thumbs up.

After our tasting he offers us a tour. He leads us down a winding stairwell to more stainless steel barrels. We all draw our own hypotheses of the various machines purposes based on the different shapes, Italian signs and dials. He explains each of their purposes to George who relays the process of removing the grapes skins to all of us.

We are led into another room that is filled

with crates of wine piled from the floor to the ceiling; there must be over a thousand bottles of wine. We look at each other with wide eyes, imagining having such a collection at our own disposal. Stocks of corked barrels fill another room. The crimson dripping stains around huge wax corks look like bullet-hole wounds.

Back upstairs we meet the owner's wife, Luisa, who is equally knowledgeable about the wine and olive oil making processes. Luisa shows us the olive oil machines, much smaller than those dedicated to transforming the grapes.

She explains the process of making oil in slow Italian to me. I nod my head every few minutes and say, "Si," feigning comprehension.

For the bottling process she uses her hands to help explain, holding an imaginary bottle, pouring in imaginary wine and topping with an imaginary cork. She is standing in front of a machine that we learn costs about 300,000 dollars.

I look at her Salvatore Ferragamo sunglasses and her husband's LaCoste T-shirt and wonder if it's a lucrative business.

Luisa leads us outside into another building where we follow her upstairs to a room that resembles a restaurant. Various half full bottles of wine and grappa are laid out on a front table.

She pours us a glass of wine that resembles port. It's strong and there is nowhere to spit it out. I am unaware of the customs of wine tasting.

After she pours us each of us a glass of white wine, apologizing that it's not "freddo," she briefly leaves the room.

A blackberry tart is in her hands when she returns she is apologetic once again that it is all she has for our spur of the moment tasting.

As we sip our glasses of sweet white wine we follow her out on the balcony surveying the Italian countryside.

"Mia casa" she says proudly pointing to an adjacent balcony covered with potted plants and a brightly colored mosaic door.

I picture what its like to live her life. Perhaps she has an eligible son.

- Philly Petronis

It was a pleasure!

THERE IS A RESTAURANT ON Numana Beach called Les Parasols.

Between the restaurant and the shore is a seating area of wooden tables and dark wicker chairs. Don't try to sit with you feet on the chair because a manager will come outside and say slowly but in perfect English, "I have to ask you to put your feet down."

The simple yet classy restaurant plays Norah Jones over the speakers. There are mostly tables for two with a few exceptions that seat four.

In Italian class we learn that macedonia means fruit salad and this restaurant serves it. The refreshing snack - a collection of diced fruits - is in a pitcher with a lid and it looks fresh as can be. You can also order a single, whole apple if you prefer. They serve it on a plate with a knife, fork and napkin, further proof of the restaurant's elegance.

Other food that is available for lunch is salads, small chocolate cookies and pizza squares.

There was a young waiter at the restaurant and he was practicing his English with us.

"After you say thank you and I say it was a pleasure is that it? Does it end?" he asks.

"Um, yeah," Ann answers.

He hands the bill over and Ann says, "Grazie."

The waiter responds, "It was a pleasure!"

Then he throws his head back laughing, sending his curly black locks bouncing about in rhythm with his chuckling.

- Caitlyn Slivinski

The future of publishing...today!

Apprentice House is the country's only campus-based, student-staffed book publishing company. Directed by professors and industry professionals, it is a nonprofit activity of the Communication Department at Loyola College in Maryland.

Using state-of-the-art technology and an experiential learning model of education, Apprentice House publishes books in untraditional ways. This dual responsibility as publishers and educators creates an unprecedented collaborative environment among faculty and students, while teaching tomorrow's editors, designers, and marketers.

Outside of class, progress on book projects is carried forth by the AH Book Publishing Club, a co-curricular campus organization supported by Loyola College's Office of Student Activities.

Student Project Team for *Andiamo Le Marche*:
    Caitlyn Sliviniski, '07

Eclectic and provocative, Apprentice House titles intend to entertain as well as spark dialogue on a variety of topics.

Contributions are welcomed to sustain the non-profit press's work and are tax deductible to the fullest extent allowed by the IRS.

To learn more about Apprentice House books or to obtain submission guidelines, please visit www.ApprenticeHouse.com (made possible by the generous support and creativity of Mission Media). To order Apprentice House books, call 410-617-5265 or fax 410-617-5040.

www.ingramcontent.com/pod-product-compliance
Lightning Source LLC
Chambersburg PA
CBHW041528220426
43671CB00002B/18